What people are saying about *Mailbox, U.*

"What do dragons, cowboys, and tin men have in common? Not much you'd think, but all are part of an eclectic mix of 'mailbox art' to be featured in an upcoming book to commemorate the 100th anniversary of rural free delivery."

Teresa Eubanks
The Calhoun Liberty Journal
Bristol, Florida

"Traveling the back roads and blue highways photographing America's most unique mailboxes, Rachel Epstein has gotten a close look at this nation's soul."

Terry Anderson
Green Bay Press-Gazette
Green Bay, Wisconsin

"Delivering the mail to 133 rural boxes can be either a challenge or a joy. One certain box that gives me a lift is the iron cowboy that almost says, 'Howdy!'"

Bill Bock, rural letter carrier
Lebanon, Kansas

"After word went out in a newsletter to postal workers about Epstein's search, she was barraged with photos of unusual boxes on their routes. The boxes express something about the person's life, occupation, hobby, or sense of humor."

Elizabeth Wasserman
The Mercury News
San Jose, California

"We want to voice our encouragement of your project. It is important and timely; as a society we are beginning to appreciate the extraordinary ways that ordinary people use ordinary objects to communicate personal experience."

Susanne Theis, executive director
The Orange Show
A Folk Art Foundation
Houston, Texas

"I think what Rachel is doing is legitimizing and validating mailbox art as an American folk art. I think she's memorializing America's love affair with the mail."

Dan DeMiglio, manager
U.S. Postal Service
Corporate Relations Center
San Bruno, California

about the author

Rachel Epstein is a professional photographer who studied painting at the San Francisco Art Institute and later apprenticed in a photo studio before starting her own business. She began photographing unusual mailboxes in 1990. Since completing *Mailbox, U.S.A.*, her work has expanded to include varied aspects of postal service. She is recognized for her sensitive photo portrayals of people from different cultures, lifestyles, and environments. Her photographs have been published and exhibited throughout the country. Rachel lives in the San Francisco Bay Area and is working on her next book.

MAILBOX, U.S.A.

Stories of Mailbox Owners and Makers:
A Celebration of Mailbox Art in America

Stories and Photos by Rachel Epstein

GIBBS·SMITH PUBLISHER

SALT LAKE CITY

99 98 97 96   5 4 3 2 1
Text and photos copyright © 1996
by Rachel Epstein
Illustrations copyright ©1996
by Ben DeSoto

This is a Peregrine Smith Book,
published by
Gibbs Smith, Publisher
P.O. Box 667
Layton, UT 84041

Design and composition
by Lezlie Sokolik
Stories and photographs throughout
this book by Rachel Epstein
Editing and craft directions
by Caroll Shreeve

Printed in Hong Kong

Library of Congress Cataloging-in-
Publication Data

Epstein, Rachel, 1962–
Mailbox, U.S.A. :
Stories of Mailbox Owners and
Makers: A Celebration of Mailbox
Art in America / stories and photos
by Rachel Epstein ; craft illustrations
by Ben DeSoto.
p. cm.

Includes sources and index.

ISBN 0-87905-701-7
1. Mailboxes–United States–
History. 2. Mailboxes–United
States–Design and
construction–Pictorial works. 3.
Rural Free delivery–United
States–History. I. DeSoto, Ben.
II. Title.

HE6497.M3.E67 1996
383' 145' 0973—dc20   95-46330
                                      CIP

Contents

Acknowledgments

*This book is dedicated to Sandy and Lee Epstein,
known to me as Mom and Dad.*

Everyone who has been part of my life for the past five years understands the passion with which I have pursued my mailbox book project. From day one, I've had the support of my family, friends, acquaintances, and people I have never met.

I'm pleased to recognize the many people who participated in the development of this book. James H. Bruns, director of the National Postal Museum, was especially helpful in guiding my initial research on mailboxes in America. Dan DeMiglio, manager, and the staff of the U.S. Postal Service Corporate Relations Center in San Bruno, California, were instrumental in promoting my efforts to find

extraordinary mailboxes. I value the help of postal service employees who assisted in the search. I'm grateful to Candice Fuhrman, my literary agent, who believed in me and guided me through my first book proposal. Charles Fuhrman, who worked with me on the original design, passed away before this book was completed. I always looked forward to our brainstorming sessions, and I miss him. Gibbs Smith, my publisher, took a personal interest in my project and was committed to its success. I was fortunate to have Caroll Shreeve as my editor. It was always a pleasure to work with her.

A heartfelt thank you goes to my friends who provided unconditional encouragement and, occasionally, waited hours for me to take "just one more picture." Anna Marks, Anna Lyubarov, Eva Wallach, and Paul Husby were especially helpful.

I want to express my appreciation to Deanne Delbridge, Suzanne Richie, and Mike Blumensaadt for sharing their photographic knowledge and wisdom.

I'd like to thank Eastman Kodak Company for their generous support.

From coast to coast, Postal Service employees, mailbox owners and makers, and U.S. Servas hosts welcomed me into their homes and communities. I will always remember their kindness. An acknowledgment goes to everyone who directed traffic around me, patiently held my reflectors, and protected my camera from the rain while I continued to work.

I'm grateful to all the mailbox enthusiasts who submitted pictures and information about unusual mailboxes. Finally, I want to thank the individuals who created the wonderful, one-of-a-kind mailboxes selected for *Mailbox, U.S.A.*

6

Introduction

In 1990, for the first time, I noticed an unusual mailbox. It looked like an airplane about to take off. Although I contemplated taking a picture of it, I decided not to waste my film on a mailbox. But, I was unable to get the image out of my mind and returned several weeks later to photograph it.

I decided to photograph other unique mailboxes and put together a small collection. By small, I meant about twelve. I had no idea then that my newfound interest would lead to leaving a full-time job, acquiring national publicity, driving nearly 25,000 miles, and creating a book that validates mailbox art as an American folk art.

"The Mailbox Project" evolved over a period of five years. At first, I looked for handmade mailboxes along back roads in and around the counties where I lived and worked. My search continued in other states during vacations; spotting an extraordinary mailbox was like finding a treasure. While talking with the owners, I realized that each mailbox had a fascinating story behind it.

I visited the Philatelic Division (now the National Postal Museum) of the Smithsonian Institution in Washington, D.C., to research mailboxes, and learned about Rural Free Delivery (RFD), which began in 1896. There were no in-depth books about unusual mailboxes. Believing a book on this subject was needed, I decided to write one to commemorate the centennial of RFD.

In 1994, the United States Postal Service and nationwide news media publicized my efforts to locate one-of-a-kind mailboxes. I chose my favorites from hundreds of snapshots sent by people from all over the country. Then I planned a 3-month-long, 18,500-mile journey from coast to coast and back again to complete the photography and interviews with mailbox makers and owners.

Each day called for covering hundreds of miles to photograph mailboxes at sunrise and sunset, the best times of day for lighting. I drove through desert heat, a snowstorm, flash floods, lightning storms, and once took shelter from a tornado. Occasionally I was wet and muddy, attacked by insects, and worked in the path of oncoming traffic. Yet, I appreciated the ever-changing climatic conditions and found beauty in each environment.

When I began this book project, I had no idea how deeply into the heart and soul of America it would take me. Everywhere I went, people welcomed me into their homes and shared their wisdom and life stories. It is a joy to be able to share so much of what I discovered on my journey for *Mailbox, U.S.A.*

I set out to photograph handmade mailboxes and, in the process, discovered America and the creative spirit of its people.

Rachel Epstein

A Short History of Rural Free Delivery

by Bil Paul
U.S. Postal Service
Corporate Relations Center
San Bruno, California

James H. Bruns,
Director of the National Postal Museum
Smithsonian Institution
Washington, D.C.

If you lived on an American farm during the 1800s, life could be austere, especially when it came to communicating with your neighbors and far-off relatives. The telephone hadn't come into general rural use yet, and radios were merely a fantasy. To learn what was happening, you generally had to harness your horses to a wagon or carriage and ride many miles into town. There, along with buying provisions, you could share the latest gossip and pick up your mail at the post office.

Around the turn of the century, farmers joined forces with politicians, especially through the popular farm organization of the day—the National Grange—and made it known that, like folks in the larger cities, they wanted their mail delivered by letter carriers. There were objections—Congress fretted about the cost, some postmasters and townspeople were worried about losing their small rural post offices, and express companies and small-town store owners predicted a loss of business.

But rural free delivery (RFD), like rural electrification, was an idea whose time had come. With typical American energy, agents were sent out to map the countryside and plot mail routes. Dusty, dirt roads that turned into expanses of mud in the spring were improved so that rural carriers could navigate their routes.

The first rural letter carriers delivered to a bewildering array of mailboxes—everything from lard cans to cigar boxes. When the sometimes motley mailboxes deteriorated, carriers were required to tell the owners to improve them or mail service would be stopped. After one carrier left such a message, he reported that he ". . . came pretty near to getting lynched." Eventually, the Post Office Department designed two sizes of the now-famous tunnel-shaped rural box, one for letters and a larger one able to receive packages. As of 1916, all newly installed boxes had to have the approved design (unless the postmaster granted an exception).

Rural letter carriers were a durable breed. In the early days, delivery from horse and carriage meant toughing it out along muddy roads and during storms. In the north, the often bitterly cold snow season meant difficult traveling. On some days, routes were completely impassable. It wasn't surprising that rural carriers were quick to try the first motor-driven vehicles, but they often broke down. There were no tow trucks to come to the rescue. Rural carriers operated veritable post offices on wheels, selling stamps, money orders, and postage for parcels.

Due to RFD, the lives of rural people improved. With the daily delivery of newspapers, magazines, and catalogs, farmers kept in touch with advanced farming methods and the world beyond the horizon. After parcel post was introduced to the mails—which farmers played no small role in bringing about—country folks could shop anywhere in the world.

As the twentieth century progressed and farm mechanization made great inroads, the ratio of farmers to city dwellers decreased. The advent of radio and television lessened the cultural distinctions between country and city. Even though our current technology provides the ability to communicate by E-mail and fax, many people still have a special relationship with their rural letter carriers and with the mail—as evidenced by their beautiful, custom-designed mailboxes.

Uncle Sam

U ncle Sam, to us and so many Americans, is a symbol of our country. That's why I thought it would be appropriate to build an Uncle Sam to hold our mailbox.

Kids had been driving down our street and hitting mailboxes with a steel bar or a baseball bat. We replaced our mailbox three times in less than three weeks. One day, our mailbox was scattered all over the ditch by the road. Then, we decided to put up something that was sturdier.

I call our Uncle Sam full size although he's only about five feet tall. His arms are held out to hold our mailbox, which is made from 1/4" sheet metal. I drew Uncle Sam on a piece of cardboard, and my husband, Ron, used that as a pattern to cut it out of 1/2" sheet metal. I painted Uncle Sam and put white reflector stripes on his hat. At night the stripes shine and I can see my way home.

My husband and I are very patriotic. Ron was in the Marine Corps during the late '50s and early '60s. He works for the Department of Defense and belongs to the American Legion. He also belongs to the Brothers of Vietnam, a motorcycle club. They're supporters of the Vietnam War, and most of them are veterans. I think it is patriotic to support your country in an unpopular war.

We try to have the flag out for all the holidays. To us, being patriotic means that you're loyal and proud of the country you live in. You do everything you can to make it a better country. I think it means you cry every time you hear "God Bless America."

Donna Kailey
Cheyenne, Wyoming

False Teeth

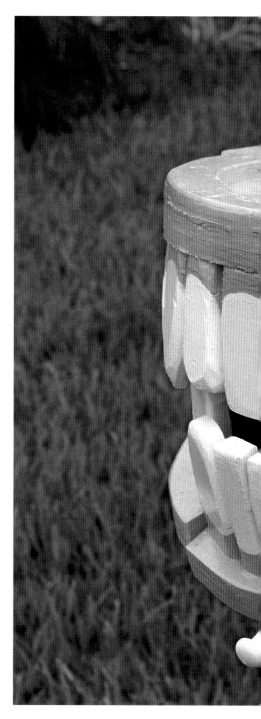

> "When I first drove up and saw this mailbox, I started laughing. I couldn't believe it. It was hysterical. It made me feel great." —*Larry Bercu, Miami, Florida*

I've been making teeth for the last 26 years. I make about 20 sets a week, and I thought it would be appropriate to make a mailbox that showed what I do for a living. There wasn't much thought involved. I just decided to make it on the spur of the moment. I cut the teeth out of scrap wood that I found in the garage. The front teeth are incisors, and the back teeth are premolars and molars. I didn't put a full complement of teeth in, but there's enough there to show exactly what the mailbox represents. I screwed and nailed the teeth together, painted the mailbox, and put it out in front of the house.

I probably have the only mailbox that ever bit a mailman. It was originally designed to be opened from the top. Apparently, when the mailbox was first installed, the mailman reached inside and it slammed down and cut his arm slightly. I came home to a letter from the postmaster, telling me to remove my mailbox because it was a hazard. Instead, I redesigned it. Now, the bottom jaw opens rather than the top, and it can't bite the mailman anymore.

From time to time we give the mailbox a prophylaxis. We use a paintbrush to clean and whiten the teeth. It has dentist appointments about once every six months.

A lot of people stop and look at our mailbox. There are even tour buses that go down our street and stop in front of our house so that everybody can see our mailbox.

When we call the Chinese restaurant where we order our takeout, we just say that we're the house with the teeth, and they know exactly where to deliver our food.

All of our neighbors seem to like our mailbox, even though it doesn't go with the large homes in this elegant ranch community. Last year, we went to a neighborhood crime-watch meeting. It was basically an introduction so we could meet

everyone. We told them that we lived in the house with the teeth. One of our neighbors blurted out, "We wanted to one-up you. My husband is a cardiologist, so we were going to make one into a heart." I told her, "Good thing he's not a proctologist." Our neighbors started to laugh so hard that I thought they were going to die. That broke the ice.

Fred Gelfand
Davie, Florida

Owner/Maker: Dell Weston Location: Santa Fe, New Mexico

Dinosaurs

OWNERS: Jean and Roger Graham   MAKER: Kathleen G. Thometz   LOCATION: Mendham, New Jersey

Dragon

OWNER: Gael G. Jarrett   MAKER: Paul Baker   LOCATION: Chardon, Ohio

OWNER/MAKER: Ronald Denning LOCATION: Graham, Washington

Lebanon Cowboy

We're just a mile south of the geographic center of the 48 states. This is a pretty peaceful place to live. We're mostly farmers and ranchers out here—real friendly people. Everybody knows everybody; it's like a big close-knit family.

We do a little farming here. We have a few cows and some pigs. My husband Dean's main job is managing the co-op grain elevator.

When we bought this place from Linda Dinkel in 1984, the cowboy mailbox was already here. Her son, Jeff, made it at the "vo-ag" [vocational agriculture] school here in Lebanon. At the time, there was nothing around the mailbox, and I thought it would be appropriate for the cowboy to have a fence behind him. Then I planted flowers to spruce it up and just kept adding things such as the horse harness. I thought it would look good with the cowboy. Dean had to throw a little barbed wire up there, too.

The mailbox represents the past when it was easier for farmers to make their living. It's as if the cowboy's just sitting out there; and he's

OWNER: **Pinky Hunter**
MAKER: **Norman (Pappy) Hunter**
LOCATION: **Grand Junction, Colorado**

so peaceful, rocking back and forth in the wind.

I wish the people in the big cities would see what farmers really have to put up with. They ought to have to come out one day and do what us farmers have to do, so they can understand how we put food on their table. They go to the grocery store and think food comes in a can or a box. One time we were loading hogs out there in the rain. It was lightning and thundering and we thought, this isn't worth getting killed over. We're not getting anything out of it.

There's not near as many farmers as there were twenty, thirty years ago. The big companies and big farmers are getting bigger, and we just can't compete. We're already talking about getting out of the

hogs. While we hate to give up what we've worked so hard for, the only way we can stay alive is to get out. I don't know what we're going to do now. We have some cows, and we're going to try and stick with those for awhile. Dean's job gets us through the tough times.

Some day, it'll get better. It's got to get better. We work hard and are determined to survive. We always have. We just have to keep that in our minds. We don't have to raise hogs all our life. There are other things that we can do and be happy with. This is the land of opportunity. It really is.

Yvonne Oliver
Lebanon, Kansas

Plowman with Horse

When I moved to Hidden Corral Ranch, I found a potato digger in the yard. I thought it would make a good mailbox holder. It was here for awhile, until a guy, returning home from work at about four o'clock in the morning, fell asleep at the wheel. He drove through all our flowers and ran over the potato digger, scattering the parts over 150 feet.

After I collected the parts and brought them into my shop, I spent a few evenings tinkering. I re-assembled the remnants of the potato digger to look like a plow. Then, I built a man to sit on it. I turned the mailbox into a horse that pulls the plow.

We dubbed the man Plowman. His body is made out of a 15-gallon barrel and his head is a milk jug. I made his nose and ears out of some putty. He's wearing old clothes and a straw hat. I've had to change his clothes over the years. Some of the shirts and shoes have been mine, and I think we got the coveralls from the Salvation Army.

All our horses have contributed to this mailbox. My wife, Marty, occasionally takes a little bit of tail hair from Jake, Lady, Bea, Buba, and Mariah when she grooms them. We've needed hair to cover the back of Plowman's head and for the horse's mane.

OWNER: Lester Gross   MAKER: Curly Leiker   LOCATION: Hays, Kansas

I was proud of the old mailbox but I'm prouder of the new one. I've never been unhappy that the potato digger was run over. Then, it looked important and impressed people. They would say, "I know where you live. You live by the mailbox that sits on a potato digger."

Since I've rebuilt my mailbox, people stop here every time they break down, run out of gas, have a flat tire, or whatever their problem is. They come here because the mailbox looks so friendly and they think we are, too.

Hank Court
Bend, Oregon

Stiffney or Bust

My Dad had a lot of influence on me when I was growing up. He was a teacher and an X-ray technician, but his dream was to be a cowboy. He was never quite able to fulfill that dream. I always wanted to be a cowboy, too. So, I did a lot of phone calling and letter writing until I got on a big ranch in eastern Wyoming. I got some experience as a ranch hand there, and on ranches in North Carolina and Georgia. I just kept working for different outfits and finally got inspired to buy my own place.

I've fulfilled one dream in my life and that is running my own ranch. I'm fairly capable of the jobs that we have to do here. I pride myself on the fact that I grew up in town and, yet, I know as much about ranching as people who grew up with it.

Our mailbox is a covered wagon. It was made by my father-in-law, Jim Ogle, and given to me as a gift. It commemorates that we've been on this ranch for fifteen years now. On the side of the mailbox, it says, "Stiffney or Bust." There have been several times that we almost went bust. I guess my father-in-law is well aware of the struggles it takes to make a ranch successful. He's a wheat farmer and, when he was a young man, had the same problems we have now.

Our ranch is about three miles outside of TenSleep, a small, slow-paced community. It's got that western aura about it, and has always been a cowboy town. This is a typical Wyoming ranch in that we run both cows and sheep. We trail the livestock up to the Big Horn Mountains for the summer. They stay there until the middle of October. Then, they come off the mountain and go out to the Badlands until December, when they return to our ranch for the remainder of the winter.

It's hard work, but I believe in what I'm doing. It's a good way of life. We give the Lord a lot of credit for us still being here, because we've made a lot of mistakes and yet we're still kicking.

Mark Stiffney
TenSleep, Wyoming

Grain Truck

OWNER: **Darrell Unrein** MAKER: **Curly Leiker** LOCATION: **Hays, Kansas**

Garbage Truck

OWNER: **Dennis Hickey**   LOCATION: **Old Field, New York**

Monster Truck

For six years, I raced monster trucks all across the country. My mailbox represents one of those trucks, the Copenhagen/Skoal Crusher. It's about 4 feet long and 2 feet high. The tires are 18 inches high. It's got a light bar on top, flags in the back, and the same paint scheme as my truck had. The front opens up for the mail. As far as I know, I have the one and only monster truck mailbox.

A monster truck is an oversized pickup. Its tires are about 5-1/2 feet tall, and it's got a big hopped-up motor. In a race, there are two sets of cars, five cars in one set and ten in the next. When the green light comes on, you nail the throttle and hit the first car. That puts you up in the air, sometimes 15 feet above the cars. You clear the rest of the cars and land in "no man's land" between the two sets. Then, you nail the throttle again, hit the first car of the second set, and fly over the others to the finish line. When you land, it's a pretty good jolt. You don't even know where you are for a split second.

When you're driving a monster truck, you've really got to have a cool head. There are so many things that can go wrong while you're riding on that cutting edge. You block out everything else and your heart goes about a thousand miles an hour. You get that old adrenaline going when you fly over the cars and win the race. At a big show, there are 50,000 to 70,000 people watching and cheering you on. When the race is over, there are times that I'm shaking so badly I can't even unbuckle my helmet. Fans come down from the stands and ask for autographs. The kids get a big kick out of it. I guess I'm just a big kid because I get a kick out of it, too.

People relate to monster truck shows in America. They like to see action and a good wreck. The more you get sideways and out of control, the louder the crowd cheers. You can see all the car crushing and glass flying, but nobody gets hurt. It's good family entertainment. To me, that's what it's all about.

Yeah, I guess I do pray a little bit when the national anthem is playing and everybody's singing along. I bow my head and ask the man upstairs to take care of me, the truck, and everybody around. You could say I'm patriotic. America is the best country in the world, and I'm proud to be a part of it.

Warren Davis
Nine Mile Falls, Washington

Dump Truck

My mailbox looks like a dump truck. It says "R. Hicks Construction" on the side, although I'm not really in the construction business. I'm a barber.

I've always been interested in construction, and I love to build things. Most of what I've built can't be seen by people driving by. So, I thought if I made an unusual mailbox, everybody would see it.

For five years, I used a crane and dug a two-acre pond. I leveled out the dirt with a bulldozer and planted 6,000 walnut trees. When I considered making a mailbox, I thought about making one that looked like a crane or bulldozer. But, a dump truck seemed easier, because its engine compartment could hold the mail.

The dump-truck mailbox was made from 1/4" and 3/16" steel. The paint, called "Powder Coat," is the same kind used on some motorcycle frames. A friend of mine, who owns a Harley-Davidson shop, took my mailbox, along with some frames, to Chicago, where it was painted. I bought the boat trailer tires from a farm-supply store.

My mailbox has headlights, taillights, and even inside lights. The

GI Joe figure inside the cab is also lit up. It's often dark when I get home from work, but, with all these lights, I can see the mailbox and the mail inside.

I always have radios playing in the house, garage, and in the barn. It makes people think there's someone home. My mailbox also has a radio that's on all the time. I figured one more wouldn't hurt.

This type of dump truck is used in gravel pits and limestone quarries to haul boulders to the crusher. One limestone quarry allowed me to go to the bottom of the pit and pick out whatever I wanted. I looked at

about 400 boulders and, finally, found one with a flat surface for my truck to sit on. It weighed in at 5,000 pounds. I also weighed the dump-truck mailbox, which was 460 pounds, before I filled the back with rocks weighing 15-to-20 pounds each.

A lot of people think that I really work in construction. Maybe I should've gotten into the construction business rather than barbering. But, I like what I'm doing.

Richard Hicks
Union Mills, Indiana

Cow and Cowboy

We had lived in our house for 17 or 18 years, and the original mailbox was quite decrepit. For the last year or two, my neighbors had been sending me anonymous notes suggesting that the mailbox looked tacky and maybe I should do something about it.

I decided to take a welding class to pursue my interest in working with metal. That seemed to lend itself to making some kind of mailbox. I wanted to do something that had a western theme, since Phoenix is a western town. The idea of a mailbox in the form of a cow evolved.

The class was attended by all males who worked on rebuilding cars. They would walk by my cow and say, "Mooooo." There were only a couple of us, both attorneys, who were interested in the artistic end of

things. Midway through building the cow, I decided to make a cowboy to complement it. I cut him out of one 4-by-8 piece of sheet iron. He stands about 5 feet tall from his oversized hat to his boots, is barrel chested and bowlegged.

When the project was completed, I installed it and hid it under a cover. Then I invited my neighbors to

attend the dedication ceremony for my new mailbox. About 20 people stood around enjoying champagne, crackers, and fruit as I made a little speech. I thanked them for inspiring me to build a new mailbox and apologized for the years of having an unsightly one. Then I pulled the cover off! What seemed like moments of silence—probably only 10 or 15 seconds—was followed by polite applause. Many people scratched their heads, wondering what this was that they now had to look at.

The final irony about the mailbox is this: a visiting cattle rancher from Colorado viewed the mailbox and said to me, "It would take a lawyer to build a mailbox that included a cowboy and a cow, and make the cow a dairy cow and not a beef cow."

Dennis Wortman
Phoenix, Arizona

Log Cabin in New York

When we were kids, my parents brought us up to the Adirondacks for family vacations. We stayed in log cabins that were very rustic. We'd water-ski in the day, and at night we'd roast marshmallows over a campfire. Sometimes we'd see black bears. I dreamed I'd have a log cabin in the Adirondacks when I grew up.

The Adirondack Park is a beautiful, forever-wild area. It's mountainous and has lots of pine trees and lakes. My husband and I bought property here, thinking we were just going to camp on it. Instead, we built a log cabin-style house. Our friends helped us build it from start to finish. It took us about three years. We have a mailbox that is a replica of our house, with the red roof and log cabin siding. The log cabin makes me reminisce back to when I was a little girl on our family vacations.

It's really nice to wake up early, just before sunrise. We can hear the cries of the loons on the lake and their echoes in the mountains. In the early evening, we usually sit at the end of the dock, behind our house, and fish for bass. The ducks swim by and climb up on the rocks, where they sleep for the night. We watch the sun go down, and in the darkness of the night, we often hear the eerie sounds of the coyotes howling. Living here is definitely fulfilling my lifelong dream.

Betsy Bain
Mt. Pleasant, New York

Log Cabin
in Wyoming

I'm employed by the Park County Sheriff's Department and am the resident deputy for this remote mountain area. Mail service here is once a week on Thursdays. We do get a lot of heavy snow, and I've seen the road up here closed for three weeks at a time. Sometimes it can be pretty rough getting in and out of here. When it gets that way, mail may be a day late or it could be several weeks late.

My mailbox is a replica of an old log cabin. It used to belong to a very dear friend of mine by the name of Lee Luckinbill who built the mailbox about 1951. Lee ran a small logging sawmill operation in the area. Since he was a logger, I guess he decided he needed a log cabin mailbox.

The gentleman who was carrying the mail at that time complained to Lee about the mailbox. He thought it took too much effort to lift the roof off to put the mail in. That made Lee so mad that he took the mailbox down and nailed up an old barrel in its place. After Lee passed away in 1981, I became the owner of the mailbox and have used it ever since.

I can remember Lee talking about the wintertime in the '30s and '40s. When the road was closed, he was here alone all winter. People normally didn't get mail then. Sometimes, if the groceries ran a little low, he'd take off on horseback with two or three pack horses and go into town. A lot of times, he would check with the neighbors to see if anybody wanted anything. I can remember two things that he said people always wanted, some fresh produce and more whiskey.

I've talked to a lot of the old-timers and heard their stories about this area. I wish I had been born many years earlier so I could live back in those times. I would have liked the remoteness and the way of life they had then. That way of life is gone.

I love it here. There aren't many people around. The closest neighbor is probably a good five miles away in one direction and ten miles in the other. I guess I just like the isolation.

The deeper the snow gets, the better I like it. When it snows, the beauty of the area changes continually. The ground can get tracked up throughout the day, but during the night we'll get fresh snow and everything will be covered up again.

In the winter, there are thousands of elk here, quite a few moose, and deer. It's my favorite time of year.

Dan Estes
Sunlight Basin, Cody, Wyoming

Log Cabin in Maryland

Back in '88, I started making miniature log cabins. I've also built four log cabin mailboxes that are all in use today. I made these mailboxes because I was interested in making them. It's not something I can put my finger on and say, "This is the reason." It's just something I wanted to do, that's all. I am very proud of these mailboxes. I'm the only one who makes them.

I found the materials out in the woods where beavers had been. They had chewed the lower branches off some trees, right up to the trunks. The new growth was perfect for building my mailboxes. After I went out "logging," I trimmed the "logs" to the right length. Then, I soaked them in water and wrapped them up in a wet towel to keep them pliable. You have to keep them pliable so that you can nail them together. The refrigerator down in the basement is full of these "logs" and little boxes of worms for fishing. I used real chinking between the "logs" and cut all the shingles out of wood. Everything is real.

Nobody taught me how to make these mailboxes. I just said I was going to do it and I did it. Teaching yourself, you just say, "I'm going to do it." So, you go ahead and you try. You do your best and if it comes out right, good. If it comes out wrong, you start all over again.

I often think about early settlers who used their ingenuity to create what they needed to live. They had to make everything from scratch, and logs were their building material. I've always admired their will to survive.

Bob Probst, Sr.
Baltimore, Maryland

Since the pictures of the mailbox were taken, a few months ago, my Dad passed away. Three nights after he died, our mailbox was vandalized. He never really taught me how to build a mailbox, step by step. But, I would visit with him while he worked on one project or another, and I absorbed what he was doing. Fortunately, there are some "logs" and shingles in Dad's refrigerator that I can use to repair the mailbox. I'll still need to go out into the woods to do some "logging."

In a way, I think it's appropriate now, because Dad always felt closer to God out in the woods than in a church. He said, "God didn't make the church, but he sure made the woods." It will be nice to be out in the woods, getting "logs," and remembering Dad. He lived and died with great dignity. And we're going to miss him a lot. We're always going to love and remember him.

Kathleen Florian
Perry Hall, Maryland

Bear with Beehive

I'd been noticing mailboxes and wanted one that would be different from everyone else's. I thought a bear would be right at home here, but none of the bear decorations I saw anywhere suited me.

My husband, Nemo, and I were having lunch at a restaurant in Hogansburg, a town on the St. Regis Indian Reservation, near the Canadian border. My placemat had a picture of a bear on it. Nemo said, "Suzanne, here's your bear!"

We took the placemat home. Nemo copied the picture of the bear onto a 4' x 8' plywood board and cut out the silhouette. Then, we painted the mailbox brown and yellow to make it look like a beehive. The bear looks like he's trying to steal the honey. We got this idea for our mailbox from hearing stories about folks around here who raise bees for honey. They have to watch out for bears who will destroy their beehives.

We're located on the edge of the Adirondack Mountains. You'll see bears by the roadside all through this area. So, when people see this bear by the mailbox, they think they're seeing a real bear. They slam on their brakes, stop, and take a look. Hundreds of people take pictures of the bear, and some beg Nemo to make one for them. Even a minister stopped in once and said, "I'll pay the price that you want for it." I refused. I said, "There's no price. I don't want anybody else to have a bear like mine. "

Suzanne Stevens
Harrisville, New York

Covered Bridge

When we bought this property in Weaverland Valley, we needed a mailbox. I decided to build a duplicate of Weaver's Mill Bridge, a covered bridge that was built in 1878. It was named after the Weaver family who had a cider mill down by the creek. The people in this valley are, primarily, Mennonites, although there are a few Amish families. The Mennonites and Amish both use horses and wagons. It's all agriculture out here —corn, tobacco, and alfalfa.

We get along very well with our neighbors and can always count on them. We do a lot for each other. There are times when they bake a pie, cake, or cookies and bring them over, just because they want us to enjoy them.

Weaver's Mill Bridge was one of the reasons we fell in love with this area. We named our property "Covered Bridge Acres" because of the covered bridge. Even though the bridge doesn't belong to us, it is near the corner part of our property.

The mailbox was built to be a miniature version of the bridge. It was made out of exterior plywood and painted the same colors. Both have cedar roofs. I even hand-painted the signs that tell people the maximum height and weight that the bridge will take. The mailbox was mounted on a split-rail fence so that it fit in with the area.

The mailbox as it is today is not identical to the bridge. It's eleven years old now and, because of some very heavy western winds, snow, and ice, has weathered harshly.

One time, we lost it when a hurricane came through. The mailbox and the whole fence were washed into the corn field. We searched and searched but couldn't find them. Our neighbor, Luke, came down and said that he, too, had lost some things. He went over to the cornfield to look for them and came back dragging a few of our fence posts. We were so sad because our mailbox was gone. Luke went back to the field and looked again. He came out with this mud-packed blob and said, "I think this is your mailbox." We started cleaning it up and, sure enough, it was our mailbox minus all the paint and most of the cedar shake shingles. We restored it and put our mailbox back on its perch.

Dennis Draves
East Earl, Pennsylvania

Golden Prairie Baptist Church

It takes intention to get to the Golden Prairie Baptist Church because it is not on the way to anywhere. Its neighbors, now, are mainly grain fields of wheat and barley and cattle pastures. The nearest town, which is Burns, is fourteen miles away.

Our mailbox was built by Jim Ogle, who is in our congregation. He made it in the 1950s as a model of the original structure here. The mailbox is very simple in design, as was the church building. It represents the simplicity of the community. The people here don't go for a lot of frills. They do what needs to be done and pitch in when a neighbor needs help. The original structure, as well as the addition and parsonage, were built by men of the church.

Above the mailbox door are three letters, REV, which stand for reverend. Although that is my profession and title, the word *reverend*, to me, is divisive. I believe a title such as that gives too much credit to me and not enough to God or Jesus. So, I choose not to use it, and also encourage my friends and the congregation not to use it when they address me.

Many people in this community are employed in agriculture and as teachers, truck drivers, or other secondary occupations. They have to supplement their income because agriculture is in difficult times.

This area is subject to very harsh weather. In the winter, blizzards have shut us down for as much as two weeks. In a severe blizzard, with swirling snow, you can not see and immediately become disoriented. In the fall, we get high winds that can loosen tumbleweeds in the fields and cause fences to break down. This is also a severe hail belt. In the late spring or summer, a hailstorm could come through here and completely destroy all the crops in its path.

But, that mailbox was well built and has survived every storm. I think it represents this community in the sense that it is efficient and down to earth.

Jim Brown
Burns, Wyoming

OWNER: Avis F. Thompson   MAKER: Jean Sparin   LOCATION: Awendaw, South Carolina

Bread

My grandfather, Captain John Derst, came to the United States from Germany in 1856. Shortly after arriving in New York, he booked a passage on a steamer, which docked in Savannah, Georgia.

For two years, my grandfather worked with his family in shoe manufacturing, but that business was not for him. He went to work in a bakery. His plans to start his own business were interrupted when the Civil War broke out. Eventually, he became a chief baker and made bread for the troops in Atlanta. After the war, he returned home to Savannah. In 1867, he started his own bakery.

My father bought the bakery from him in 1917. Over the years, he built it up into a pretty-good-sized business. I bought the business in 1965, when he died, and I've had it since then. I've got two sons who are following me; this will be the fourth generation.

All my life, I've thought that a mailbox looks exactly like a loaf of bread. As I got interested in the baking business, I considered making mailboxes that looked like our loaves of bread to be used as advertisements on the highways. I didn't pursue it because I'm not in the business to make mailboxes for others.

Our mailbox looks just like the most popular loaf of bread we sell, which is Captain John Derst's Good Old Fashioned Bread. We painted the mailbox and, of course, we had to make the wrapper ponytail where it opens. We made that part out of fiberglass. When people see my box, I want them to think, "Buy our bread rather than somebody else's." I thought the mailbox would be an acceptable form of advertising for our bread.

Everybody in this locale knows Derst Baking Company. We employ about 500 people and make about 200 different products. These are distributed within a 150-mile radius of Savannah. Most bakeries these days are owned by conglomerates or huge bakery chains. We're unique in that we're still an independently owned bakery. Our family owns it, and we plan for it to stay that way.

Edward J. Derst, Jr.
Bluffton, South Carolina

Milk Carton

Rosenberger's Dairies has been a family operation since 1925 when raw milk was shipped to processors in the Philadelphia area. Then, in the early '30s, the family started a raw-milk route to Hatfield, delivering milk and other dairy products to the customer's door. It was in 1936 that my dad moved the milk business and his family to the west end of Hatfield, our present location.

Ever since that time, it's been a lot of hard work for my family and local people. Dad said he needed a dairy so he could support the family, including his ten children. He believed if we didn't make much money, at least we'd have plenty of milk to drink.

Our dairy has grown along with the community. At the time we started here, there were many farms surrounding us. Presently, only one is left. We are now reaching out as far as 20 miles to purchase our milk from about 58 farmers. Then, we process and package it for customers within a 70-mile radius of Hatfield. We use 125 vehicles to deliver our dairy products, fruit juices, and spring water in Pennsylvania, Delaware, and New Jersey. We still make home deliveries.

The old mailbox located in front of the dairy didn't have much character. The idea of a new milk carton mailbox was to catch people's attention as they drove by and to duplicate the design, color, and print of our product. It is approximately 5 feet high and shaped like our quart milk cartons. Many people have said, "That's quite a unique mailbox you have there."

Now, after about 8 years, it's old hat around here. But it's still a useful mailbox. I tell visitors who need directions to Rosenberger's Dairies to take Forty Foot Road toward Hatfield until they see the milk carton mailbox.

Marcus Rosenberger
Hatfield, Pennsylvania

Corn Cob

We grow a lot of corn around here. Out in the fields this time of year, the corn is ready to plant. When it comes on up, we'll be pulling it and selling it.

I saw a picture of a corn cob mailbox in a catalog. I'd never seen another and had to get one. After I ordered it, they wrote back saying they weren't going to have any more. And the next day the mailman rang the bell to deliver the mailbox. Neighbors said that's the first time they'd seen a corn cob mailbox. They asked me what I wanted with it. I told them that I wanted something different from anybody around. And I like that on wet days no water gets inside the box, so the mail stays dry.

When people in town need directions to our farm, we tell them to look for a big pine tree in the yard and the corn cob mailbox on the left-hand side. That's how to find us.

Donald Cox
Fort Barnwell, North Carolina

Morton Salt

OWNER/MAKER: **Harold T. Morton** LOCATION: **Albion, New York**

The Cake Lady®

I wanted to be an art teacher or a commercial artist, but I wasn't able to go on to high school and college. This was the time of the Great Depression, and my folks didn't have any money for books and clothing. So my sister, Charlotte, and I traveled together in show business for 12 years.

In 1947, my husband, who was a postman, got a transfer to California. Then, everything went up but his salary. We couldn't pay the bills, and I knew I had to do something. I went into cake decorating so that I could work at home and be with my daughter. For 5 years, I baked in the day and decorated at night. Then, I had one job after another in 14 bakeries around Los Angeles.

Over the years, I introduced American-style cake decorating in eight countries, did promotions in nearly every state in America, and was a guest on TV talk shows. Everywhere I went, I was called the cake lady. Other people are called the cake lady also, but I'm The Cake Lady®. In recognition of my

achievements, the International Cake Exploration Society inducted me into their Hall of Fame in 1985.

I'm 76 years old now and still going strong. A few years ago, I had a vision that we needed a cake museum, and now it's a reality. My Mini Cake Museum has guest teachers, a reference library, and tours. As far as I know it is the world's first cake museum.

I couldn't put up a sign for the museum, since it is located in a residential area. I decided that a cake

mailbox would do the trick. Now, people can find us easily.

Cakes are a symbol of celebration. I think they show love and caring. We have cakes for baby showers, birthdays, anniversaries, and other occasions. Even though we don't eat cake with every meal or every day, what's a celebration without a cake?!

Frances Kuyper
Pasadena, California

OWNER: **Mike Crayton**   MAKER: **Warren Basher**   LOCATION: **Hockessin, Delaware**

OWNER: Mary Milkovisch MAKER: Ron Milkovisch LOCATION: Houston, Texas

John Deere Tractor

My stepson, Bruce, loves farming. He farms 1,500 acres of wheat and cotton, with the help of his 19-year-old son. Like many farmers in this part of the country, he likes to do things his way.

I spent about four months building a mailbox for Bruce. Since he uses John Deere equipment, I knew I had to make the mailbox resemble his tractor.

I used a little model of a John Deere tractor to go by. I painted it green and yellow using original John Deere paint. Nothing is welded on. The cab portion is made from thin

OWNER: **W.H. (Bill) Hammer** MAKER: **Rick Whiteman** LOCATION: **Clarksville, Texas**

sheet metal that I cut out with hand snips and fitted together. The box is a regular mailbox, the seat is a solid block of wood that I hand carved, and the steering wheel is a shut-off valve from a water faucet. I picked up the wheels at a junkyard. They came off some kind of farm implement. I tried to make the mailbox as realistic as I could.

Bruce likes anything that identifies him as a farmer. He told me this mailbox was one of the best presents I could give him because it represents what he does and is proud of.

Calvin O. Stoner
Randlett, Oklahoma

OWNER: Michael Werth MAKER: Chris Werth LOCATION: Hays, Kansas

OWNER/MAKER: Dave Traylor LOCATION: John Day, Oregon

OWNERS: Becky and Dennis Hillyer
MAKERS: Marcie and Richard Dyer
LOCATION: Bayfield, Colorado

Tin Man

I am A. O. Doughty. I am known as the Tin Man because I'm in the tin business. It's an interesting business and I've been in it a long time. In fact, this coming March, I will have owned and run this company for thirty years. We work on cotton gins, oil mills, grain elevators. . . . We manufacture everything here and cover seven to eight states. It is not just a little two-bit tin shop, is what I'm trying to tell you.

My mailbox at home was run over by a vehicle. I had to build a new one and got to thinking about it. I said, "Well, I'll build me a tin man." So, I did. I used component parts that we manufacture here to build it. The oil can is the actual mailbox.

It feels real good to create something that is accepted like this Tin Man mailbox. A lot of people have really enjoyed visiting with it. I can remember when my children were going to college and brought their friends home. The first thing we always had to do was take their pictures by the Tin Man mailbox.

The mail carrier told me, "Look, A. O., this is something nobody else has got." I said, "Well, yeah. I've got an original, and I don't want anyone else to have one like mine." And, I can assure you, they don't. You know, everybody likes to have something that nobody else has got. Of course, everybody can't have the equipment and know-how to do something like this.

I design a lot of these big things that we build—the oil mills, collection systems, massive stuff—that work and do the job. But, I don't know anything about art and have never gone to any kind of art school. I don't think I am an artist. I'm really not. I didn't have a blueprint or pattern to make the Tin Man. It all came from my head how I'd want him to look. And, I thought it turned out real well. I was proud of it and that was my main concern.

Notice the Tin Man's hands. They are patterned from my hands. I took a piece of metal and drew my hands out. In a way, he's not a child of mine, but he's kind of come off some of my personality. Some of my being. And that's a hard thing for somebody to say about a piece of metal. But, he means a lot more to me than just a mailbox. What I'm trying to say is, there's a lot of myself in that Tin Man.

A. O. Doughty, Jr.
Rayville, Louisiana

Bucket Head

My mailbox can be called Bucket Head. It's definitely supposed to look like a person, although I didn't have a particular character in mind when I made it.

I wasn't working after I got out of high school, and had a lot of spare time on my hands. I always liked tinkering in my dad's garage with his welder and torches. His garage would make Fred Sandford's junkyard look small. When my parents were younger, they didn't have much and never threw anything away. So, from the accumulated stuff in the garage, I got all the parts for Bucket Head.

One day, I found a spring and leftover pipe that I could use for a body. I cut up railroad spikes and welded them into a hand. I found a tin bucket and used that for his head. I found some bolts and big nuts and used those for his eyes and mouth. The stick man wasn't preplanned but, when it started coming together, I said, "Hey, this could be a good mailbox holder."

I'm one of eleven kids. We've always been a little unique in our own way. Our family doesn't want to be like everybody else. We care about things, and we'll make an extra effort to show it. If everybody had the same house, did the same things, and looked the same, it'd be a dull society. A mailbox lets people show their individuality. If the mailbox I made brings a smile to someone's face, I get a kick out of that.

On a windy day, Bucket Head will move around a little bit, and he may catch your eye because he's not just standing there. His midsection, arms, and legs are attached to an old motorcycle spring. The first spring I used was too weak, and he bent all the way over. Then, I had to find a bigger spring and stiffen his sides. His back's a little crooked now, but it's understandable, because he's been out there a long time. Oh, gosh, I'd say, he's probably a good ten, twelve years old.

Kids go through our neighborhood and play a game called baseball. They take a bat and try to knock mailboxes off their stands. Unfortunately, Old Bucket Head's been smashed a few times. But, he got through it alright. I don't think he took it personally.

David Yoham
Miami, Florida

OWNER/MAKER: Glen Baltzer
LOCATION: Orient, Ohio

OWNER/MAKER: **David Yoham** LOCATION: **Miami, Florida**

Tin Man of Solano Road

In 1985, Ralph Ables gave birth to an idea. He decided to build a mailbox. He wanted to make it into a tin man because sheet-metal workers, and that is Ralph's trade, are known as tin men. It was a long, laborious project. Though, before I knew it, here was a new landmark, an actual mailbox that looked like a tin man.

People coming up and down the block constantly stop at our mailbox. Children play, touch, and talk to the Tin Man. The parents look around rather embarrassed and sometimes even touch and talk to him themselves. People come by on horses and stop. Our mailman absolutely loves the Tin Man.

We have lots of laughs and good times, and we've won a few awards with our mailbox. In fact, it was featured in the newspaper as one of the most unusual mailboxes in Solano County. So, he has a few things to his credit.

All over Solano County, people know that the Tin Man has been down several times because of vandalism. But, you can't keep a good man down and you can't keep the Tin Man down. So, we've rebuilt him. We've given him brand new eyes and a new paint job. He's made of solid sheet metal, and now he's filled with cement.

Hopefully he'll be standing for many years. He's become a symbol of Solano Road and the nicer things from the past that have come and gone. So, we'll keep rebuilding the Tin Man because he is Solano Road.

Mary Ann Ables
Fairfield, California

OWNER/MAKER: **Cliff Kannegieter** LOCATION: **Watertown, South Dakota**

Lou, the Muffler Man

I own a Meineke Muffler franchise. Just to be a little bit original, I figured we'd make a muffler man mailbox out of some scrap pipe and used mufflers.

Lou was born in 1983. His legs and arms were made of new pipes. We used an old muffler that came off a truck for his body. His head is a little muffler from an imported car. The actual mailbox is a muffler from an old Chevy.

The creation of this muffler man was definitely a team effort by myself, Richard Peterson, Randy Mayo, and Ray Heney. We all put our little touches onto Lou: welding the pieces together, sign writing, painting, and even putting him in the ground.

We call him Lou because the mechanics in this shop call each other Lou, just as a nickname. One guy instigated this when he started calling everybody Lou. So we welded the name "Lou" onto the Muffler Man's shirt.

Lou's had a very rough time here in Vernon. Over the years, the town has threatened to remove him. The building inspector and zoning officials consider him to be a sign more than a mailbox. Everyone has to conform to the town's strict sign ordinances and regulations. I've had many a fight over the phone, through the mail, and even in zoning meetings about the Muffler Man. The local postmaster has supported us, saying that it's a mailbox, federal property, and nobody's going to remove it.

Our mechanics have made a number of muffler men over the years. I believe we all think of ourselves as artists. There's no set pattern, and everyone has his own designs. We learn by trial and error, using the pipe-bending machine, and working on cars.

I emigrated from South Africa because of the political situation, and came to the United States in 1978. At first, I worked in construction. But, I really wanted to have my own business, and eventually started one in Vernon. Now I own five muffler shops.

I've never run across a muffler man in South Africa, South America, Europe, or anywhere else I've traveled. America is probably the only country that has them. This is such a creative country. You are free to express yourself here in many ways, including displaying a muffler man. Muffler men are definitely an American icon.

Ian Melmed
Vernon, Connecticut

OWNER/MAKER: **Doug Grote**
LOCATION: **Lincoln, Nebraska**

OWNER: Ian Melmed   MAKERS: Ian Melmed, Richard Peterson, Randy Mayo, and Ray Heney   LOCATION: Vernon, Connecticut

Harmony Filling-Station Museum

When the Harmony Cash Store was built in 1913, it consisted of a house, garage with a lubrication pit, and a small store. In 1928, it was renovated and gas pumps were installed. It was really a mom-and-pop type of place in the center of a farming community. Mom ran the store and Pop worked in the garage. He mostly repaired farm trucks and tractors. The McElravys ran this place for 46 years, until Mr. McElravy passed away in 1980.

In my retirement, I purchased the property and turned it into a filling-station museum. I'd been a mechanic all my life, so this fit right in with what I like to do. The museum has a collection of oil cans, tire-patch kits, light bulbs, several old gas pumps, plus hundreds of other filling-station items. The garage is full of tools, old car parts, and equipment from days long past. There's usually old cars sitting around here. Groups from antique car clubs come up and enjoy looking at all this old stuff.

My wife and I have been collecting car parts and things for a long while. We travel about six weeks a year, looking for things to put in the museum. Whenever we get a chance, we go to flea markets and swap meets. Any day that we're open, it's just about a safe bet that somebody's going to come here and donate an oil can or something that once belonged in a gas station.

I thought the gas pump mailbox would attract attention to my museum. It was a real chipped-up, ugly-looking thing when I bought it. I painted it and covered it up a little bit to put the mailbox in. It's an Erie pump, built around 1938. On top of the mailbox is a reproduction of the Conoco Minute Man globe, which was in use until the early '30s.

You can sit out here all day and visit with people. Old folks come in here and really enjoy it. They pick up an antique coil and know right away what it is. They like to talk about the past. What is it about these old things that people enjoy? It's the memories. Living in the past. We all do that somewhat. I do it especially bad, I suppose.

Bill Vos
Ft. Collins, Colorado

Rust to Riches

My occupation has to do with antique cars. I handle parts and restoration for customers all over the world. I use my mailbox to tell people how to get to the shop. I don't tell them to look for the address. I tell them, just look for the mailbox, turn in the driveway, and head straight on back. That works fine, except at night. Most people see the mailbox, go zipping right on past, turn around at the gas station, come back through, and come in. Being in a residential area, I didn't want to put a big sign out front. I wanted something that the old-car people would see and find of interest and in keeping with the neighborhood.

Various people have built similar mailboxes. I took the best designs of everything I saw and put them together to make this box. Many people look at it and say that it looks like a Model A Ford because of the shape of the door. The grille and headlights fold down when you open it to put the mail in. The shape of the top of the door dictates the shape of the radiator, which is a gentle curve.

I've been in the antique car business all my life and have the only restoration shop in Maryland. I don't collect mundane cars. I collect cars with histories, one-of-a-kinds, unusual cars, and limousines from famous owners. I also travel all over the world looking at cars and car stuff. Each September I conduct something called the British Car Enthusiast's Tour. We take groups of Americans over to England to visit car collections, museums, shows, and the Queen's private car collection. We do have fun!

Bill McCoskey
Silver Spring, Maryland

GAYLENS AUTO TO

OWNER/MAKER: Gaylen Long   LOCATION: Salina, Kansas

Corvette

Prior to 1953, for most people, the car was merely a vehicle that transported you from one place to another. Typically, it was not something that caused great emotion within the heart of the driver. In 1953, however, a change occurred with the arrival of the Corvette. It not only got you from one place to another but did it with dramatic style.

America's post-World War II economy was in excellent condition. Families sprouted like mushrooms in rich, fertile soil. Consequently, any car having only two seats was considered impractical. Contrary to this logic, the Corvette hit the streets with tires screeching and entered into the heart of America.

In 1953, I was only a little girl and could not possibly have known where my love affair with this car would take me.

My first driving experience with the Corvette occurred in the mid-sixties. That thrill has since been repeated many times. Getting behind the wheel, I have always felt my spirit soar. There is something about driving a Corvette that gives you a sense of being totally capable of doing anything and going anywhere. It doesn't matter if there is a destination, and the further the better. Unlimited possibilities seem to appear in the road ahead. People wave, and you wave back. There's a fascination with not only owning a Corvette but in being close to one. The Corvette has become a symbol of Americana.

In the beginning, as with any successful venture, the Corvette was only an idea. That idea, the combined dreams of Harley J. Earl and Edward N. Cole, became a reality. In 1994, thirty years after my first Corvette ride, "First Class Mail ™" also began as an idea. Combining my imagination, artistic flair, and passion for cars, I envisioned mailboxes that replicated particular automobiles. These start out as ordinary mailboxes. Each box receives a coat of primer before automotive acrylic urethane finish is added. Real chrome trim and original reproduced Corvette emblems are standard features. The people who own my mailboxes all share my love for the vehicles these represent.

My Corvette mailbox stands proudly by the road. It has not been baseball-bashed, run over, or in any way vandalized. I think one of the reasons that it has garnered so much protection is that, just like the car, there is an air of mystique, respect, and, certainly, passion surrounding it.

Terry Kohl
Randolph, Wisconsin

Guns

OWNER/MAKER: Simon (Buddy) Spight   LOCATION: Baldwyn, Mississippi

OWNER/MAKER: Bob Graham   LOCATION: Conroe, Texas

Tank

I read about some mailboxes down the road that were vandalized. I told a welder friend of mine, Brad Haberstroh, about it. He said that you have to build a mailbox like a tank, so people won't destroy it. He liked that idea, and said, "We can build one."

The tank mailbox was built right here in my garage. We worked on it in the evenings, a couple of times a week. When anybody came in, we covered it up, halted production, and worked on something else until they left. It took a little over a year to build. I'll bet you we have a hundred hours in that thing.

I tried to keep Brad from building a life-size tank. He kept making it bigger and bigger, and I had to keep him in check. It's made with nearly all used parts. Some are from old machinery that came from a candy manufacturing plant. It has about six shock absorbers underneath it and it weighs between three and four hundred pounds. I call it vandal resistant.

"Kilroy" was painted on the front of the mailbox. In World War II, wherever our soldiers went, somebody would draw a picture of "Kilroy." I guess it was a mark to

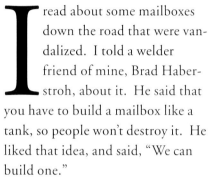

show that our troops were there. He absolutely had to be on this tank.

Neither of us were in the military or had any tank experience. But, we're both very interested in military history. Several years ago, we went down to the Aberdeen Proving Ground and saw the mile of tanks on display there. That was right after the Gulf War, before we had any idea of the tank mailbox.

My wife, Lori, told people at work that I was building a new mailbox. They all wanted to know what it was. She said it was a secret. They anxiously awaited its debut.

We put it out on Memorial Day. Everybody just loved it. People at work asked Lori, "Did your husband serve in the Gulf War?" The UPS guy stopped here a few weeks ago and asked, "Was your husband a tank commander?" She replied, "No. He just likes tanks."

Ken Smith
Colombia, Pennsylvania

Hand with Cigarette

When I needed a new mailbox about nine or ten years ago, my neighbor offered me a cedar telephone pole. Instead of making something conventional, I thought I'd make a foot out of it. Then, I changed my mind and decided to make a hand. That was a spur-of-the-moment decision. Why a hand? Well, I guess I wanted something unusual, something nobody else had. That's the way I am.

The hand was carved with a chain saw. It has a ring, which was made from pieces of flat brass. The knob is from an old-fashioned insulator. I cut the round part off and used that. The mailbox looks like a cigarette because it was in the spot where a cigarette would normally be.

We have people around here who have lots of money. In the Dunes, you can find $2,000,000 homes. I was afraid they would think my mailbox would be too outrageous for this neighborhood, but no, they loved it.

One time, I went around the neighborhood with a petition in opposition to building thirty homes across from us. These fancy people in the hills all said, "And where do you live?" I said, "I live where a hand sticks out of the ground for a mailbox." And all of a sudden, they looked at me differently. Their facial features changed, and they were much more friendly then. So, you know they can identify with something unusual. They didn't know me, but they knew my mailbox.

I'm originally from the Netherlands, but I've been an American citizen for 35 years. Although I'm still influenced by Europe, I'd say I have an American mailbox. In the Netherlands, you probably wouldn't be allowed to put that hand mailbox up in front of your house. That's why I came here. I came to the United States to have more freedom. This is a great country. People knock it all the time, but this is a great country.

Ben Conens
Holland, Michigan

Franklin Plantation

One day last summer, as me and my wife were driving by, I saw some cars parked in front of the mailbox. I thought they might have been broken down. I'm the sheriff and thought I better stop and check. I looked up and there were four girls sitting in the mailbox with near nothing on. Someone was in front of the mailbox taking their photograph. I was going to see if they needed any help, but my wife hit me on the back of my head. So, I went on about my business.

Jeff Britt
Newellton, Louisiana

When Daddy traveled to Houston on business in the late '40s, the mailbox was his landmark. It sat on top of a corner building and could be seen from a distance. It was near where he turned to go to his hotel.

One time, he noticed that the mailbox was gone. I'm sure he was having a drink somewhere and inquired about it. The owners, he was told, had gone out of business.

Daddy asked, "What happened to the mailbox?" Someone said, "It's in storage." He asked about purchasing it and was told, "You can have it if you just pay for the storage." I've heard him tell the story a thousand times, I reckon. He always said that it would have been a whole lot cheaper to have one built.

Daddy bought and sold cattle all over the country. On a trip down through Texas, he got the driver of one of our cattle trucks to put the mailbox in the back and bring it home. The mailbox has been here at Franklin Plantation since about 1956.

It has been repainted five or six times. Each time, Daddy put some variation on it, maybe his name and the name of our farm. Once, we had a sale of a new breed of cattle from Italy. He put all the sale information on the mailbox and sent postcards with a picture of the mailbox to prospective buyers.

A lot of people that we'd meet would say, "Where're y'all from?" We'd say, "Newellton." They'd say, "Oh, yeah, that's where the big mailbox is."

From the ground level to the top of the box is almost fourteen feet. The box itself is about five feet tall, eight feet deep, and four feet wide. The post is about eighteen inches

square. When they erected the thing, I reckon, they put a plate in the ground, bolted it down, and then filled the post with concrete to hold the mailbox in place. Teenagers try to chop it down with an ax. They don't succeed though. It's also been shot at a bunch of times, a thousand probably.

My son gave a speech about the mailbox at Northeast Louisiana University. To prepare for it, he wanted to ask me about the mailbox. I said, "Hell, Son, you've lived here all your life. You can make as good a story as I can."

Ben Burnside, Jr.
Newellton, Louisiana

McMailbox

The mailbox in front of our house is a replica of an old McDonald's restaurant. My wife, Marilyn, had it built for me as a gift for our 25th wedding anniversary. It represents the McDonald's of the '60s and '70s, called "the Red and White with the Golden Arches." The "Red and White" refers to the tile on the sides of the building. The "Golden Arches" were their symbol. Those were the old drive-up McDonald's where you ordered your hamburger and French fries and then ate in your car. The mailbox is pretty authentic. The door represents the area where you were served. It even has the bathrooms painted on the side.

I always wanted to own a McDonald's, but I guess I never could. So, owning a McDonald's mailbox and collecting McDonald's memorabilia are the closest things to it. Every Friday, we go to McDonald's and get their Happy Meal toy. That's a ritual. We collect memorabilia from McDonald's all over the country. If you close your eyes and somebody sets you down in a McDonald's, you wouldn't know where you were. They are all basically the same. But, when you go into tourist communities, they have different kinds of local promotional items. It's fun to collect them.

Marilyn and I visited McDonald's in London, Paris, and Rome. In Rome, the cab driver didn't know where McDonald's was located. He had to ask some people to understand what we were looking for and do a little searching, but we finally got there. It dawned on me that most Americans who go to Europe aren't looking for McDonald's. So, there are not many times a cab driver will get a request to go there. We wanted to get Happy Meal toys from a McDonald's in each country.

For many years, McDonald's had a character called Mayor McCheese. Since I'm the mayor of the city of Eastlake, that's been the label given to me when I'm teased.

Marilyn thought I would never put my McDonald's mailbox in front of our house. She thought I'd add it to our collection. At first, the kids were a little embarrassed about it. My daughter told people that we lived one house over. But, they've gotten used to it. The mailbox has grown on everybody and become a symbol of our house. When people come to this area, they know my house is the one with the McDonald's mailbox. That's fine with me. I think it's kind of fun when people refer to our house as the one with the McDonald's mailbox, and not as the house where the mayor of Eastlake lives.

Mayor Dan DiLiberto
Eastlake, Ohio

Winnie-the-Pooh

Winnie-the-Pooh was my favorite cartoon character when I was growing up. My mother tried to keep me busy, so she sat me in front of the TV and I watched Winnie-the-Pooh. It was a morning program, and I used to want to watch it every week.

I'm 31 years old now and work as a station manager for British Petroleum. Winnie-the-Pooh is still my favorite character. When my mom asked me what I wanted for Christmas, I told her I wanted a mailbox because the one I had was old and beat up. She bought me a pig mailbox from Wayne Burwell at the Mailbox Factory. I told her a pig wasn't what I wanted. So, I returned the pig to Wayne and asked if he could make a Winnie-the-Pooh mailbox. He said he could and carved both Winnie and a log out of a tulip tree. The mail goes inside the log, of course. Winnie is mounted on top and is holding his pot of honey. Eating honey is his favorite thing to do. Winnie likes to sit on logs and take it easy.

Winnie-the-Pooh is a large, jolly bear. He eats a lot and has a lot of friends out in the wilderness. That's the way I am. I'm a big, caring kind of guy.

He's wholesome, and although he's a storybook animal, his morals and values are what most people believe in. Things happen to him that can really happen to you. He respects the animals he's with— Eeyore, Tigger, and Piglet. They are inseparable. He listens to them and learns from the things they do. He is a very naive bear and makes a lot of mistakes. But, he takes them in stride and learns as he goes. He reminds me a lot of myself, and that's why I'm infatuated with him.

Winnie-the-Pooh has been around for ages. I think he's very much a part of our culture. People of all generations know him. Anybody you could say Winnie-the-Pooh to would know who you're talking about. I got my mailbox as much for myself as for the kids in the area. This is where they set up their lemonade stands now. Who knows, they might be the next entrepreneurs because of Winnie.

Is Winnie-the-Pooh a good role model? Oh, definitely! One of the best. Any kid that uses Winnie-the-Pooh as a role model is going to turn out okay.

Rich Willner
Chesterland, Ohio

Beep Beep

U.S. Mail

OWNER: **Jerry Juenemann** MAKER: **Curly Leiker** LOCATION: **Hays, Kansas**

OWNER/MAKER: Cliff Kannegieter   LOCATION: Watertown, South Dakota

OWNER/MAKER: Lee Greenberg LOCATION: Greenbrae, California

OWNER/MAKER: **Shirley Frank** LOCATION: **Key Largo, Florida**

Fishing Reel

Doug Ake walked into my sheet metal shop and asked me to make him a mailbox because he was tired of going to the post office. He kept asking me for months. I finally said, "If you stay out of my shop for a month, I'll make you a mailbox." So, he stayed away. It took me about 50 or 60 hours to build his mailbox. It's welded together from aluminum and stainless steel, mostly leftover stuff from the junkyard. The rest came from the scrap pile behind the shear.

What kind of mailbox could I make for Doug's tackle store other than a fishing reel? Doug didn't know what he was getting and didn't even ask for anything special. I wouldn't let him look at it until it was installed. When he first saw the mailbox, he could hardly believe it and asked, "How am I ever going to pay for this?" And I just said, "Don't worry about it, Doug."

Skip Johnston
Ocean City, Maryland

Our shop, Ake Marine, sells fishing tackle, marine supplies, and sportswear. We're located right on a commercial harbor by the Ocean City inlet. So, half of our customers come by boat. Our policy is, you can dock while you shop. At 5 a.m., fishermen cruise right up to the dock for bait and off they go for the day.

We have a unique mailbox that looks like a giant fishing reel. It came as quite a surprise to me, since I just asked Skip to build me a stainless steel mailbox. This is stainless. But it certainly isn't a regular mailbox.

We couldn't understand why it was taking over six months to make the mailbox. One day, the craftsman showed up with the base for it. He told me to secure it with 600 pounds of concrete and then he'd return with my mailbox. You could not believe the expression on my face when I saw workers welding the mailbox to the base. It was modeled after a Penn fishing reel, but is about 18 to 20 inches in diameter and about 2-1/2 feet wide. It has all the features of an actual fishing reel. A crank handle opens the top portion of the spool so that the mail can be deposited or removed.

Just before it came, we had given up on ever getting a mailbox from Skip. I went to the hardware store and bought a regular mailbox. We would have put it up, but it was damaged and I had to return it. In desperation, I parked my truck on the street, rolled down a window, and attached a sign that said U.S. Mailbox. I don't know if that had anything to do with the mailbox showing up the next day or not, but I imagine it did.

Doug Ake
Ocean City, Maryland

Joe's Bait 'n' Tackle

My grandfather, Francisco Garcia, was very well known as one of the greatest fisherman in Cuba. He also explored sunken ships for their treasures. I think he worked for a big American company. They hired him to explore underwater and blow up sunken ships. He used to dive for the Spanish shipwrecks of the late 1800s.

When I was seven years old, my parents flew me to the United States, and I never saw my grandfather again. When I was fourteen, my mother gave me the news that he was found drowned near the beach. It was very hard for me when I heard that he was dead. But, it was worse when I heard that he was actually murdered. I'm pretty sure it had a lot to do with the treasures that he had discovered.

I was a little boy when I lived in Cuba, but I have lots of memories. I remember my grandfather and the places where I used to hang out with him. He was a kind, gentle old guy. Very loving. Very caring. Very hard working. I loved my grandfather a lot.

Since I turned out to be a carpenter, I made a wooden mailbox in his memory. When my wife saw it, she said, "Oh, that's cute. We can put this here and that there," and I said, "No! Wait a minute. This is not, 'this here and that there.' Everything on this mailbox means something to me."

The mailbox represents the beaches, harbor, and bait and tackle shops where my grandfather hung out. There's a little wooden captain on the front of the mailbox that represents him. The shark hanging on one side represents fishing. The boat represents the little ferry that he used to steer. There's a smashed penny on part of the door that represents gold, treasure, and money. Our house number is inscribed on there, real small. There's a dive flag on there, some oars, and a Coke machine. It also has the blue and gray sky behind it. To me, the blue stands for happiness and the gray for sadness.

The lookout pirate on one corner represents me. I'm sorry, it brings tears to my eyes. It's me looking for the feeling of being young, being able to go back and be with my grandfather. It's me as a pirate because I love the sea. I'm always out there, always searching, looking for something new. To me, "pirate" is a man of the sea, a man who lives on a boat, a man who is dedicated to the sea and lives off the sea. If you sleep out there on a boat and you wake up in the morning and see water around you, you're a pirate.

We're very close to shore here, only two minutes away from the sea.

José Alvarez
Miami, Florida

OWNERS: **Karen and Paul Wiebel**
MAKER: **Jack Hamilton**
LOCATION: **Key Largo, Florida**

Fish

I was sitting in my eye doctor's office, looking at a copy of *House & Garden*. Because my eyes were dilating, everything looked blurry. I could only see the big pictures. One picture resembled a primitive, opaque, black shark. I thought I'd take a better look at it when I got home, so I cut out the picture.

When my eyes returned to normal, I took another look at the picture. The shark, mounted on a stick, was a dining room decoration. I thought, "Gee, this is nice but boring." I took the configuration of the shark, cut out a piece of antique wood, and painted it the way I wanted it to look. The piece was put on a brightly colored base. After that, I built mirrors, sculptures, and a hall stand—all with a fish theme.

Then I got a commission from an art collector to make a mailbox. While I had never made a mailbox before, the thought fascinated me. I agreed to make a whale mailbox for my client. But when I started making it, a whale didn't come out. A fierce looking fish did. It took about a month to make the piece. Its head, fins, and tail were made out of hand-painted redwood. The scales were made from strips of copper, which were treated with chemicals to bring out the blue and give it a head start on weathering. At first, I wasn't exactly sure what the fish's head was going to do. I decided it would drop down, to accept the mail.

I discovered that there was a telephone pole at the site where my client wanted his mailbox placed. He swore that he had lived here for twenty-five years and there wasn't a telephone pole there. So, we checked and, of course, there was a telephone pole. At that point, I was about half finished with the fish. So, I took off the tail and reconfigured it to look like the fish is swimming around the pole. When my client saw the fish, he was surprised and delighted.

Marvin Wies
Baltimore, Maryland

OWNER/MAKER: Nandi Devam
LOCATION: Pittsburg, California

MAKER: Marvin Wies LOCATION: Baltimore, Maryland

View Camera

When I was teaching my daughter how to drive and got to where I didn't have to hang on with white knuckles any more, I started to look around. I saw a mailbox made out of an old hot water heater. It was unusual, so I took a picture of it. As I noticed more and more unusual mailboxes, I took pictures of them, too.

My wife, Evelyn, and I would be driving down the road and all of a sudden I'd hit the brakes and pull over to the curb. She'd say, "Oh, you saw another mailbox." It's an obsession with me. I've found unusual mailboxes and stands all around the country. Although I'm just an amateur photographer, I've probably got 120 pictures of unusual mailboxes now.

Evelyn suggested that I ought to have an interesting mailbox of my own. Since I like cameras and love taking pictures of mailboxes, why not combine the two? She discussed the idea with a friend, who used to work for Kodak as a sheet-metal worker. He built an 8 x 10 view camera, which looks just like Ansel Adam's camera, around a standard mailbox. A little magnifying glass was attached to the front for a lens. The bellows were made out of sheet metal. Since the camera came out so nicely, I took it to a welder who made a tripod for me.

The handle under the camera was made from a part of a digging machine. The little brass knobs and some other parts were from electrical equipment. The tripod legs were made from pipes, which were welded together and tied into a steel plate. Since I've had trouble with vandalism, I set each leg in 80 lbs. of concrete. So, nobody is going to remove this camera.

In the last several years, I've noticed more unusual mailboxes, though a lot are commercially made. You can go to a store now and buy a mailbox that looks like a fish or a cow. But, I don't think you'll find one like mine anyplace else. This was handmade, dreamed up out of a man's own imagination.

We live in a world of conformity these days. Most mailboxes you see are standard. But, some people want their mailbox to be different from the others, so it'll stand out a little bit. My neighbors, including my mailman, think my mailbox is fantastic. In fact, a jogger came by, stopped in front of the camera, posed, and then continued jogging.

Jack Fowler
Fort Collins, Colorado

Recreational Vehicle

T he idea for an RV mailbox came as a result of my wife looking for a recreational vehicle. She looked and looked but never could decide on one and finally gave up. So, I decided to build one and told her that was the only one she'd ever get.

William J. Lewis, Jr.
Mobile, Alabama

Caboose

OWNER/MAKER: **Norman Welch**   LOCATION: **Escondido, California**

Trolley Cars

I am a trolley-car enthusiast. I came by this honestly as my maternal grandfather operated trolley cars for Capital Traction Company, and my paternal grandfather operated them for Washington Railway & Electric Company. The destination signs on my mailboxes are the routes my wife and I would have had to ride to go to our respective childhood homes from the trolley-car barn.

Robert S. Embrey
Leesburg, Virginia

ROUT

Nailbox

The mailbox, with the base-ball bat and spikes, was made when I was a student at Rochester Institute of Technology (RIT). I was studying woodworking and furniture design. A local gallery sponsored a student show of customized mailboxes.

The movie I'd recently seen was *Stand By Me*. The opening scene showed teenagers, running around in a car, smashing mailboxes with a baseball bat, a Louisville Slugger.

So, I made a deterrent mailbox, one that couldn't be smashed.

"Nailbox" has about 220 spikes on it. They are 6" galvanized spikes, all spot welded from the inside to seal and waterproof it. The bat is a Louisville Slugger, which was smashed on the top to produce a splintering effect. To get the bat on, I had to drill holes almost all the way through it and smash it on with a 15- lb. sledge hammer and a block of wood. The mailbox is 3/16" plate steel, all welded together. It is completely indestructible.

Most people laugh when they see "Nailbox." They say, "Wow, I could really use that." But, they're scared of it at the same time. They definitely know what the baseball bat is there for, 'cause in this area everybody's mailbox has been smashed once or twice.

I knew a couple of kids during high school who smashed people's mailboxes. They weren't caught, but they were chased. They were just out having a good time. Something to do in a boring small town. Like some other towns around here. Definitely. Nowhere to go. They just find something to do in their cars, like smash mailboxes and drive around fast.

Bradford McDougall
Bethlehem, Connecticut

Giant Syringe

I'm a veterinarian. I'm also 65 years old and have six kids and eight grandchildren. I love life and I enjoy what I do, treating animals large and small, here at the Wahoo Animal Hospital.

When we moved here about 22 years ago, I told my sons that we needed something to set us apart from everybody else. I told them that, with a little ingenuity, we could come up with a way of making a mailbox, like a disposable 12cc syringe, big enough for packages and a sign.

We put the mailbox up and it disappeared a few days later. I think some kids went to the rodeo in Wahoo and, on the way back to Lincoln, thought it would be fun to poke somebody with that big syringe. Who knows why? We finally located it at the University of Nebraska on the front lawn.

We put the mailbox back up. I thought I secured it better this time, but it disappeared again. A mailman happened to notice it in the garage of a house down in Lincoln. We got the police and rescued our mailbox. When we put it back up, I said, "They're never going to get it off this time."

There was another time. My son,

E. J., saw a pickup truck backed up against the mailbox. A guy cut the chains with bolt cutters, dropped the mailbox in the back of his pickup and took off. E. J. jumped in the car and raced after him, at about 100 mph. By the time he caught up, the guy must have thrown the mailbox from the pickup. E. J. quit chasing

him and returned home. Later, we found our mailbox in Swedeburg, laying on the church lawn, with the mail still in it. I have no idea why people want our mailbox.

After that time, I made this mailbox. There's no way to remove this one without a cutting torch. The box itself is well pipe, with numbers and

markings routed into it. The plunger is plastic. The door is made of old butcher block from a packing house. Straps hold the mailbox onto a cross-piece, and the post is made of oak railroad ties. I drilled a hole into the post and put a metal pipe in there, so if somebody comes along with a chain saw thinking he's going to cut the post off, uh uh. I don't think there's another mailbox like mine.

I like things that are different from everyone else's and I like to do things my own way. See what the sign up there says? We are closed when I'm not here. Otherwise, I'm here 24 hours a day, every day except when I don't want to work. I'll never turn anyone away who comes down the driveway, no matter what time of the day or night. At times, it's a little aggravating, but, then, I choose to stick with it.

Dr. William Hancock
Wahoo, Nebraska

OWNER: Bob Reed   MAKER: Wayne Burwell   LOCATION: Kirtland, Ohio

OWNER: **Vivian Case** MAKER: **Curtis Queen** LOCATION: **Citrus Heights, California**

OWNERS: Leonard and Joan Beerman MAKER: Nini Policappelli LOCATION: Los Angeles, California

OWNER: Varujan Assoian MAKER: Nini Policappelli LOCATION: Beverly Hills, California

Letter to Grandma

The inspiration for "Letter to Grandma" came during the two summers I spent in Pietrasanta, Italy, studying with Bruno Lucchesi, a world-renowned classic sculptor. Michelangelo worked in Pietrasanta with the white Carrera marble quarried from nearby mountains. The local Tomassi Foundry has been casting sculptures for centuries. World-class sculptors gather in Pietrasanta. From this international gathering, imbued with the romance of my surroundings and fellow artists, I decided to express my feelings through a sculpture of a child dressed in a country style, reaching to a mailbox to send a letter as an expression of his love to his grandmother. Now, when people look at my house and my mailbox, they know something about me, something real from a warm memory.

My journey to Italy to study sculpture with the talented and famous started unexpectedly years before. As my children were growing to a point when they could look after themselves, our family suffered a series of upsets. We moved from our home, and then my mother-in-law passed away. Four months later, my own mother passed away from a form of cancer. Within a short time after her death, I was diagnosed with cancer and, during the following seven months, I had two major and two minor surgeries. I asked my husband, "Why is this happening to us? How can we get through this?" His response was, "There is no triumph without adversity." These words became my rationale, attached to the refrigerator door with a magnet. This was my time to triumph. It helped me to reach out for a new direction and purpose.

The new direction and purpose revealed itself when I decided to take a course at a nearby university. I had never thought of myself as an artist; but, drained of energy from my recent operations, I selected a class in sculpture to quietly recuperate. Pondering what to do in my new class, I passed an Israeli dance class on my way to my own class. I saw a dancer leaping into the air, clapping her hands over her head. I thought that vision might be a good sculpture. When I first dug my fingers into the clay to capture the image of the dancer, I got the "feeling" in my hands that has stayed with me to Italy and beyond. The "feeling" was that I had received a gift from some ancestor, and that this was what I was destined to do: to put my soul into inert clay and breathe life into it. While creating this first attempt at sculpture, my new instructor was watching me, and she used her sculpting tool to write into the smooth surface of the clay, "You are very good." She underlined the word *very*. I entered "Israeli Dancer" into a museum show and received an award. My first attempt received a prize. Now, I knew what I was to do with the rest of my life.

Donna Weiser
Los Angeles, California

Boy with Mailbag

My husband, Vincenzo Tozzi, is a retired professor of philosophy and history. He was born in Italy and settled in Rome, where he established two schools. After forty years in Rome, with the Roman and Hellenic influences, he tends to like statues and columns.

I'm an American. I was born and raised here. After Vincenzo and I were married, we decided that part of the year we would live here in Lafayette, California, and the other part of the year we would have to be in Orvietto, Italy, for the harvest and the wine. We have vineyards near Orvietto and were importing wine to this area under the Tozzi label.

About 12 years ago, Vince went to Rome and saw a statue. You'll find many of these statuaries there. He saw this mailbox, fell in love with it, and sent it over to California with a shipment of wine.

We believe our mailbox was styled after the typical nineteenth-century mail carrier of Northern Italy. He's carrying a mailbag, and his horn is to announce the arrival of the mail. He probably delivered the mail on foot and was taking a rest, sitting on a wine keg.

My carrier was very unhappy with the mailbox because he felt that it would be an inconvenience for him. He'd have to get out of his mail truck to put the mail in. A disagreement ensued. After the passage of 6 or 7 years, he entered our mailbox in the Walnut Creek Mailbox Beauty Contest. I forgot all about it, but then, a couple of months later—we won! It was a fun experience, and we became friendly with our carrier again.

Rena Tozzi
Layfayette, California

Air Mail

OWNER: Jerry Stark
MAKERS: Denise, Brian, and Dale Stark
LOCATION: Santa Rosa, California

OWNER/MAKER: Russ Thompson LOCATION: Richmond, California

Mail Truck

OWNER/MAKER: Wiley T. Garman   LOCATION: Manassas, Virginia

The Denton Mailman

I needed another mailbox that people would notice because they didn't seem to see the one I had. They kept knocking it over and I had to keep pushing it back up. So, I thought if I made a guy, they would try to stop running him over. At least sixteen and maybe eighteen years ago, I made The Denton Mailman. However, some people evidently don't even look when they back up and he's been knocked flat about three times. But, he's tough.

His body is made out of twelve-inch-diameter, half-inch-thick wall pipe. His neck is made out of three-inch pipe, his head from about six-inch pipe, and his nose is a piece of half-inch metal. For the baseball cap, I wrapped a piece of flatbar around his ears, cut out a top, and rounded it a little before I welded it on there, and cut out a brow. Some of the girls around here asked if they could paint him blue. I said, "Fine with me." Then, someone tore off his legs. I just stuck on some white box tubing that I happened to have and said, "Good enough."

I started out as a rodeo rider. When I got out of school, at 14, I rode bareback broncs and bulls in the rodeo circuit, all around the country. Somewhere around 1954, I was buying, selling, and shoeing horses. I was also into cars and hot-roddin'. I got so many speeding tickets, that the judge told me I would either have to join the service or go to jail for about ten days, pay a $300 fine, and lose my license. So, I went into the Air Force and was the crew chief of a fighter plane in the 317th Fighter Squadron. That was the end of my cowboy life for awhile.

When I came back from the service, I shoed horses in the day and played saxophone in a band at night. Rock and roll, country, whatever they wanted to hear. Then, one day, my buddy said, "I wonder if you could help me out for a couple of days. I'm short of help." I said, "Cool with me." He said, "You know how to weld, don't you?" I never welded before in my life. I said, "Yep." It was either weld or work a shovel, digging forms out, and I thought welding would be the way to go. So, I learned real fast and I've been welding ever since.

Billy Ray Lockerman
Denton, Maryland

Lady in Waiting

My name is Andrew Vajna. I was born in Hungary and migrated to the United States in 1956. I made Los Angeles my home, where I live in a great neighborhood between the Valley and Beverly Hills, hidden from traffic and smog.

I'm a motion-picture producer credited with the Rambo series starring Sylvester Stallone, and *Total Recall* with Arnold Schwarzenegger. I've made a host of other films in the past and am working on several for the future.

One Christmas morning, I walked outside to look for Santa and I saw this new mailbox. Lo and behold! It was sitting in the place of the old mailbox. It was a gift from Gabor, my school friend from 30 years ago. I thought it was a great idea and have been enjoying it ever since.

The mailbox was made by Nini Policappelli, an artist and designer who makes mailboxes for the rich and famous. He says the only thing that crossed his mind when he created this design was a lady waiting for the mail.

Andrew Vajna
Beverly Hills, California

Anyone who's driven the back roads of America knows what a folk-art form mailboxes have become. The mailboxes reflect their designers' individuality, America's continuing love affair with mail, and friendly relationships with letter carriers. The U.S. postal system is this country's original information superhighway—a network connecting everyone from Alaska to Key West, rich or poor, six days a week. Mail is the medium that allows recipients to touch and feel the message. Because of this intimacy—even in the age of the telephone, fax, and Internet—the amount of mail just keeps increasing, year after year.

Dan DeMiglio
Manager, Corporate Relations Center
U.S. Postal Service
San Bruno, California

As I drive along the back roads of America, on photo assignments and vacations, I'll be looking for roadside mailboxes. Perhaps some will be new creations inspired by Mailbox, U.S.A. I can imagine cake, cellular phone, and log cabin mailboxes sprouting up like wildflowers. These creations are sure to delight all who see them. I invite readers to write to me about one-of-a-kind mailboxes they have seen or made, including a picture and the address of each mailbox. I'd like to consider them for inclusion in a sequel to Mailbox, U.S.A.

Rachel Epstein
P.O. Box 513
Mill Valley, CA 94942

Resource Guide
to mailbox artists

Name: . . . .**José Alvarez**
Address: . . .9660 Caribbean Boulevard
Miami, FL 33189
Phone: . . . .(305) 238-3833
Style of mailboxes: . . . . .handmade by
carpenter; wood and
meaningful treasures
See example on pages 80–81

Name: . . . .**Wayne Burwell**
Business: . . . . .Mailbox Factory
Address: . . . . .7857 Chardon Road
Kirtland, OH 44094
Phone: . . . .(216) 256-6245
Style of mailboxes: . . . . .anything
imaginable: animals, vehicles, buldings;
hand-carved, painted, or airbrushed
See examples on pages 70, 73, 94

Name: . . . .**Ben DeSoto**
Business . . . . .DeSoto Design
Address: . . . . . . .1093 East 4875 South
Ogden, UT 84403
Phone/Fax: . . . .(801) 479-9492
Style of mailboxes: . . . . .painting on
standard mailboxes or wood
constructions
*See examples throughout the idea section,
all drawings on pages 115–43*

Name: . . . .**Nandi Devam**
Business: . . . . .Tile Art
Address: . . . . .3761 Rolling Hills Court
Pittsburg, CA 94565
Phone: . . . .(510) 427-0149
Style of mailboxes: . . . . .tile art
See example on page 82

Name: . . . .**Earle (Skip) Johnston**
Business: . . . . .Metal Magic
Address: . . . . . .12748 Sunset Avenue
Ocean City, MD 21842
Phone: . . . .(410) 213-0001
Style of mailboxes: . . .metal fabrication,
large-scale replicas
See example on pages 78–79

Name: . . . .**Curly Leiker**
Business: . . . . .Curly's Metal Art
Address: . . . . .2398 Codell Road
Victoria, KS 67671
Phone: . . . .(913) 628-8161
Style of mailboxes . . . . .welded figures;
recycled materials
See examples on pages 18, 22, 74

Name: . . . .**Bradford McDougall**
Address: . . . .84 Middle Road Turnpike
Woodbury, CT 06798
Phone: . . . .(203) 263-3966
Fax: . . . .(203) 263-4234
Style of mailboxes: . . . . .whimsical
constructions; welded steel
See example on pages 90–91

Name: . . . .**Ian Melmed**
Business: . .Meineke Discount Mufflers
Address: . . . . . . .374 Hartford Turnpike
Vernon, CT 06066
Phone: . . . .(860) 875-0438
Fax: . . . .(860) 232-6326
Style of mailboxes: . . . . . .muffler men,
women, and animals; aluminized
exhaust pipe and mufflers
See example on page 55

Name: . . . .**Kathleen G. Thometz**
Business: . . . . .Hand-Painted by
Kathleen G. Thometz
Address: . . . . .18 Orchard Street
Mendham, NJ 07945
Phone: . . . .(201) 543-9679
Style of mailboxes: any design–scenes,
florals, masterpiece reproductions;
hand-painted
See example on page 13

Name: . . . .**Marvin Wies**
Address: . . . . .48 Penny Lane
Baltimore, MD 21209
Phone: . . . .(410) 486-0918
Style of mailboxes: . . . . . .very colorful,
sometimes whimsical; wood, metal, and
unusual materials
See example on pages 82,83

Name: . . . .**Donna Weiser**
Address: . . . . . . .277 S. Spalding Drive
Penthouse #401
Beverly Hills, CA 90212
Phone: . . . .(310) 201-0216
Style of mailboxes: . . . . . .abstracts and
representational figurative sculptures;
bronze and other materials
See example on page 99

Index of Photographs

**The *original* information superhighway—
and considerations for designing your own mailbox to put alongside it**

Dear *Mailbox, U.S.A.* readers:

I'm delighted that Rachel Epstein has chosen to celebrate mailbox art. She's a very determined woman who became intrigued with the genre and travelled the entire country photographing the most interesting mailboxes around. I guarantee that after you've looked through her book, you'll never see a mailbox in the same light again.

Anyone who's driven the back roads of America knows what a folk-art form mailboxes have become. The mailboxes reflect their designers' individuality, America's continuing love affair with mail, and friendly relationships with letter carriers.

I like to point out that the U.S. postal system is this country's original information superhighway—a network connecting everyone from Alaska to Key West, rich or poor, six days a week. Mail is the medium that allows recipients to touch and feel the message. Because of this intimacy—even in the age of the telephone, fax, and Internet—the amount of mail just keeps increasing, year after year.

If you're inspired by this book to create your own unique mailbox, the U.S. Postal Service, would like you to incorporate some design parameters for purely practical reasons. This will help you pass the muster with your local postmaster who should approve your mailbox before it's pressed into service.

• So that your carrier will have easy access, position the bottom of your box 40 inches above the pavement or ground. The recommended support pole for a mailbox is a 4" x 4" wood column or a two-inch-diameter metal pipe, buried two feet. Don't build a mailbox system so massive that it might cause injuries if a vehicle ran into it. Finally, if you live in snow country, mount your box on an arm, four feet out from the support pole, so that snowplows can plow under and next to it.

• The mailbox should have a durable "flag" that when raised, indicates mail is present to be picked up.

• Some other common-sense items: the box needs to be large enough to receive small parcels, shield the mail from adverse weather, and have a door that opens and closes easily. Display the house or box number on the side of the box in numerals more than one inch high (or on the front of the mailbox if among other boxes). The design should be in good taste.

Enjoy the book and good luck with your project!

Dan T. DeMiglio

Dan DeMiglio
Manager, Corporate Relations Center
U.S. Postal Service
San Bruno, CA 94099-8000

Contents

Plans, Directions, and Options for Making an Unusual Mailbox

Text for this section is by Caroll Shreeve, illustrations are by artist Ben DeSoto, whose mailbox talents are noted in the Resource Guide to Mailbox Artists on page 110.

Log Cabin

Basic Box: Log Cabin
Materials & Tools:

Thin, fresh, pliable sapling "logs"
Plywood sheets, 1/2" thick
Wood glue
Paint brush/varnish
Hinges (2)
Hammer/nails
Screwdriver/screws
Electric or handsaw

Design submitted by Bob Probst, Sr., whose mailbox and story appear on page 31.

How-to Tips:
Inner Box

1. On a pretty day, go out into the woods and with a sharp knife, cut the first new growth on the trees (diameter a little bigger around than a quarter). Make sure the logs have bark and are free of bugs. Cut 38 logs 20" long, and several extra for mistakes. Take along a big bag or a grandchild to help carry the logs home.

2. Soak logs in water for two days, drain, wrap in a damp towel, and store in the vegetable crisper of your refrigerator.

3. Saw a wood floor 15" x 6-1/2"; two sides 13-1/2" x 5-1/2"; front and back 6-1/2" x 6-3/4" angling up to support the roof.

4. Assemble inner-box pieces with wood glue and small nails.

Log Exterior/ sides

1. Remove logs from crisper only as needed. Cut 6 logs—3 of them 18-1/2" long; 3 of them 16" long.

2. Alternate long and short logs on the table, with the longest one on the bottom when assembling sides. If making windows, cut them out 3-3/4" from each side and allow 3-1/4" between them. Cut pieces for both sides before gluing and nailing individual logs to the plywood box.

Log Exterior/ front & back

1. Cut 6 logs—3 logs 9-1/2" long, 3 logs 7" long. If you want a door, cut it 2-1/2" from each side for a door measuring 3-1/2" x 2-1/2". When gluing and nailing front and back, the shortest log goes on the bottom.

2. Attach floor to sides, front, and back using screws.

Roof

1. Cut 2 pieces of plywood 10-1/2" (for overhang) x 19-1/2". Assemble with wood glue and nails.

2. Out of thin plywood, cut 162 shingles 1-1/2" by 3/4": 27 shingles in each row, 3 rows to each side of the roof. Glue to roof.

3. When dry, support the inside of the mailbox lid roof with 3 logs: one 16" long on the inside center, two 18-1/2" long on the inside at the base of each long side.

4. Outside, under the peak of the roof, use four logs to fill the space; in lengths: 7", 6-1/2", 4-1/2", 2-1/2".

5. Attach the roof to a "cabin" wall using a pair of 2" hinges, each having holes for three screws that secure the bottom inside log of the roof to a top log of a cabin wall.

6. Affix a 13" chain to the back of the roof from the opening side to prevent the roof lid from coming loose as the mail is put in and removed.

7. Varnish with three coats of outdoor varnish.

Personal Touches

1. Cut plywood to fit windows and doors; make window frames and shutters.

2. Add a doorknob, stones for the chimney, a flag, flower planter, cat on the roof, your name and address.

3. Use weatherproof caulking compound for log chinking.

4. Attach securely to a post with long screws.

Covered Wagon

Basic Box: Covered Wagon with Variations
Materials & Tools:

Standard rural-delivery
  mailbox, secured to a post
Wheels, found or created
Drill/bolts
Screwdriver/screws or welder
Hammer/nails, or epoxy glue
Weatherproof paint/brushes

How-to Tips:

1. Paint an existing mailbox or purchase a new one. Suggested colors: white for "canvas" top; red, brown, or green for "wood-look" wagon bed; black or red for wheels; red for flag.

2. Hand paint or nail on metal numbers and letters for name and address, U.S. Mail, or other desired information. Weatherproof hand-painted information by painting over wording with two coats of clear polyurethane varnish.

3. Wheels may be rubber, cut sheet metal, or found-art circles, painted and attached with screws, bolts, nails, or epoxy glue. If the wheels don't have spokes radiating from the axles, painting lines to represent them will carry off the wagon-wheel effect. Knobby bolts at the axle point (even if only glued on with epoxy) give a more realistic antique-wagon appearance.

Personal Touches:

1. The addition of ropes, barrels, and luggage, a metal or wooden hitching tongue on the front, kids, dogs, and toy horses pulling the wagon can create more "crossing the prairie" imagery on your covered-wagon mailbox.

2. For a soap box derby, use "racer" wheels or modify recycled training wheels off of a two-wheel bicycle. Paint on racing stripes in hot colors and add decals; convert the flag to a steering column or hand brake with paint, and your Cub Scout or Derby Day racer is ready to roll.

3. Minus the wheels, the basic box offers endless possibilities with a little imagination and some paint. In this book you may have already noticed the loaf-of-bread

mailbox. It could have as easily become a hoagie, hot dog, or submarine sandwich.

4. A rolled-up newspaper can be created by decoupaging actual newspaper pages to the box and leaving the wheels off. This suggestion gives new life to an old battered box that only requires a fresh look. Weatherproof with two coats of clear polyurethane varnish.

5. By following the shoe mailbox directions (pages 132–33) and adjusting the tube shape to attach at the front of the box, a chimney for an old-fashioned steam train can be created. Attach a metal bar between the wheels. Altering the sizes of the paired wheels so that the bars appear to work in tandem will add authenticity. A metal or plastic cowcatcher in front and a window painted on for the conductor will complete the antique steam engine.

Book

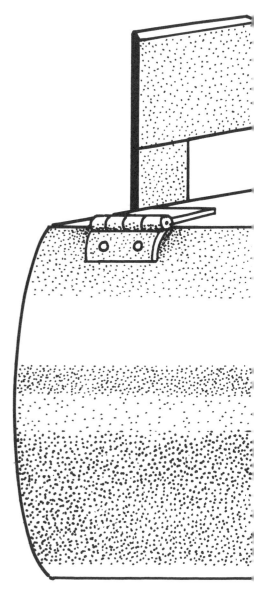

Basic Box: Book with Variations
Materials & Tools:

Plywood sheets, 1/2" to 3/4" thick
Electric or handsaw
Hammer/nails (option)
Screwdriver/screws
Wood glue
Weatherproof paint/brushes
Hinges (2 or 3)

How-to Tips:

1. Create a paper pattern to resemble a book, with its front cover on top to be the lid. Trace the pattern pieces onto plywood and saw out the shapes needed to create the box. For the lid, have enough of a lip overhang to be gripped easily. Note that the illustration shows the mailbox from the back, so that the spine of the book and its hinges can be seen. The mailbox has a believable book-cover appearance because the top and bottom of the box extend a little beyond the sides.

2. Join the box pieces together with wood glue and nails or screws. Allow to dry; then sand and wipe clean.

3. Attach the lid of the mailbox with 2 or 3 hinges.

4. Paint your name and address on the side of the book mailbox that is most visible to your mail carrier. Then, paint fine, straight lines on the sides that resemble the pages of the book.

5. The book's cover may be any color you prefer. Consider matching the trim on your home. Weather seal with clear polyurethane varnish or weatherproof paint.

6. Attach the completed book mailbox to a sturdy post using brackets underneath screwed to both the box and the post.

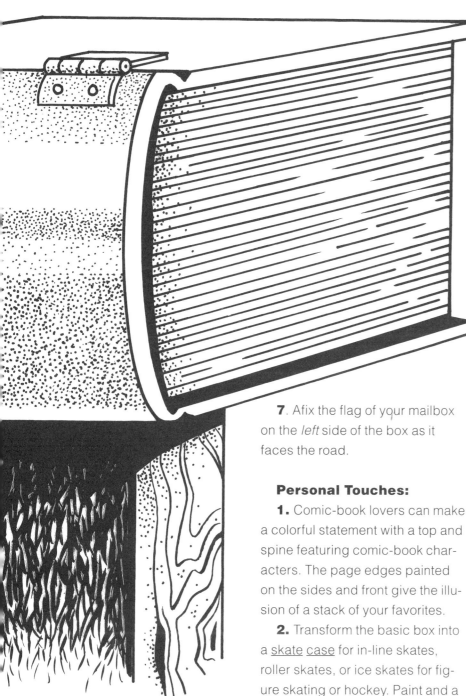

7. Afix the flag of your mailbox on the *left* side of the box as it faces the road.

Personal Touches:

1. Comic-book lovers can make a colorful statement with a top and spine featuring comic-book characters. The page edges painted on the sides and front give the illusion of a stack of your favorites.

2. Transform the basic box into a <u>skate</u> <u>case</u> for in-line skates, roller skates, or ice skates for figure skating or hockey. Paint and a recycled skate-case handle will give the desired effect. Adding an outgrown skate that has been filled with craft resin to maintain its shape, allowed to harden, then weatherproofed with clear polyurethane varnish before being attached to the lid will leave no questions asked about what belongs in the case.

If a roller skate is used, drilling through the box lid and into the wooden or hard plastic wheels will be an effective means of bolting the skate to the mailbox.

The other varieties of skates will no doubt require metal brackets and screws. To attach the skate across its arch, secure a brace under the shoe sole to the lid of the mailbox.

3. This basic book can be enhanced to be "about" any idea with your choice of recycled hobby and occupation items, from computer parts to toy trains. Weatherproof and attach to the mailbox lid.

Flamingo

Basic Box: Flamingo with Variations
Materials & Tools:

Standard rural-delivery mailbox

Sheet metal/tin snips or
metal shears, vice grips/vice

Wrought-iron rods or
recycled rebar

Metal strips or brackets,
bolts, washers, and nuts

Screwdriver/screws or welding
supplies and equipment

Weatherproof paint/brushes or
airbrush

See Lee Greenberg's Flamingo Mailbox on page 76.

How-to Tips:

1. Securing a 4-1/2' length of iron rod or recycled rebar in a vice, bend it slightly at about the half-way point with vice grips and a hammer. Welders will have the necessary expertise and equipment to heat the rods to make bending for "knees" easier to accomplish. Form a pair of angular water-bird legs, keeping in mind that flamingos are among the birds whose legs bend in the opposite direction from ours.

2. Bend the top ends of both legs at right angles and securely fasten them to the base of the standard metal mailbox with screws and metal strips, or brackets, or by spot welding the strips to the base of the box. Make certain that the angle of the bird's knees is opposite to the angle of the top of leg attachments. Plan the angles so that the box tilts toward the mail carrier's truck window. Before making all mailbox angles permanent, try using a folded newspaper and some bulk mail to test the reliability of inserting and retrieving mail without it falling on the ground or into the lap of the mail carrier who drives up in a truck.

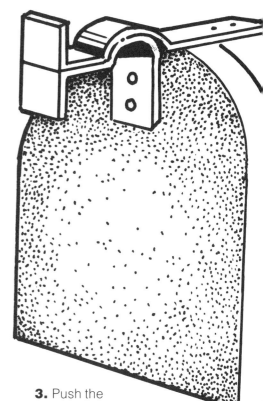

3. Push the "feet" ends of the legs into a tree stump bored with appropriate-sized holes oozing with epoxy glue, or into a metal lid in which you have bent and secured the ends of the leg rods before filling the lid with quick-set fiberglass or cement.

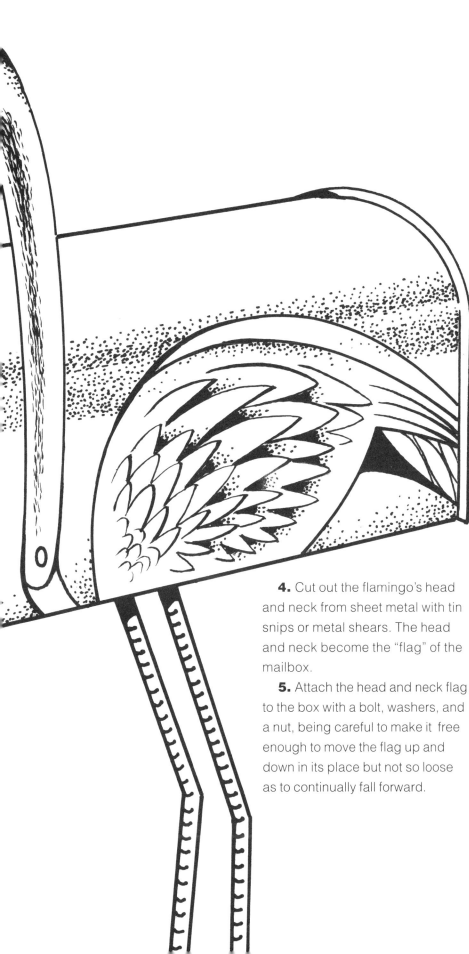

6. Sheet metal may also serve as the basic material to be formed into curves and made into wings, then attached to the box with screws or by spot welding. Wings and other details may also be painted on.

7. Paint the flamingo pink with weatherproof paint. Add a black dot for an eye on each side, name, and address.

Personal Touches:

1. With a new paint job and a few adjustments to the head and neck "flag," a <u>stork</u> , a <u>great blue</u>/<u>white heron</u>, or an <u>ostrich</u> can be made.

2. Sheet metal wings will require sizes and shapes unique to each bird species. Consult books or visit an aviary.

3. Make the neck longer, add a second pair of metal-rod legs, paint tan and put on <u>giraffe</u> spots. Giraffe knees work like our knees.

4. Cut out the flamingo's head and neck from sheet metal with tin snips or metal shears. The head and neck become the "flag" of the mailbox.

5. Attach the head and neck flag to the box with a bolt, washers, and a nut, being careful to make it free enough to move the flag up and down in its place but not so loose as to continually fall forward.

Aquarium

Basic Box:
Aquarium/Terrarium
with Variations
Materials & Tools:

Plywood sheets, 1/2" to
3/4" thick

Electric or handsaw

Hammer/nails

Screwdriver/screws

Wood glue

Weatherproof paint/brushes

Hinges (2 or 3)

Pipe post

Plastic or metal strips,
or masking tape (optional)

Clear polyurethane varnish/
disposable brush

How-to Tips:

1. Transfer rectangular pattern shapes for the basic top-opening mailbox onto 1/2"-to-3/4"-thick plywood. Saw out the shapes.

2. Using wood glue on all joints, attach the sides of the box to the base, and nail or screw the pieces together. Woodworking experts may want to add a rabbet near the top inside surface of the box to act as a seat for the lid, if they choose to set the lid inside. The option is to rest the lid on top of the mailbox sides. (Setting the lid inside the box is not recommended for climates where frequent rain or seasonal snows will mean soaked mail or frozen-shut lid.)

3. Sand and finish the top edges of the mailbox, the sides, and opening edge of the lid. Attach the lid to the side of the mailbox with 2 or 3 hinges. A handle for opening is recommended.

4. A flag for this aquarium mailbox might resemble a box of fish food or a frog.

5. Make the aquarium edges look like the metal strips that hold tank glass together. You may choose to create the illusion with paint. You may use metal, wood, or plastic stripping in a 1/2" width and secure it with epoxy to each of the edges, mitering for neat corners. Paint if necessary as most fish tanks have black metal edges

to hold the glass together.

6. Paint the round post blue for water to match the "water" in the tank, and add white circles of various sizes to give the illusion of air bubbles. Repeat some on the sides of the box so your sea creatures can "breathe." Don't forget the details such as plants, shells, coral, and toy castles to make your mailbox more realistic.

7. Paint at least two coats of clear polyurethane varnish over the entire surface of each side that represents glass.

Personal Touches:

1. Using the same basic box shape, transform the aquarium into a terrarium with frogs and turtles, or exotic creatures such as snakes, lizards, iguanas, and tarantulas. Include plants, food, and water dishes. White or blue paint that is too light to be water may serve as the color of the "air" inside the terrarium.

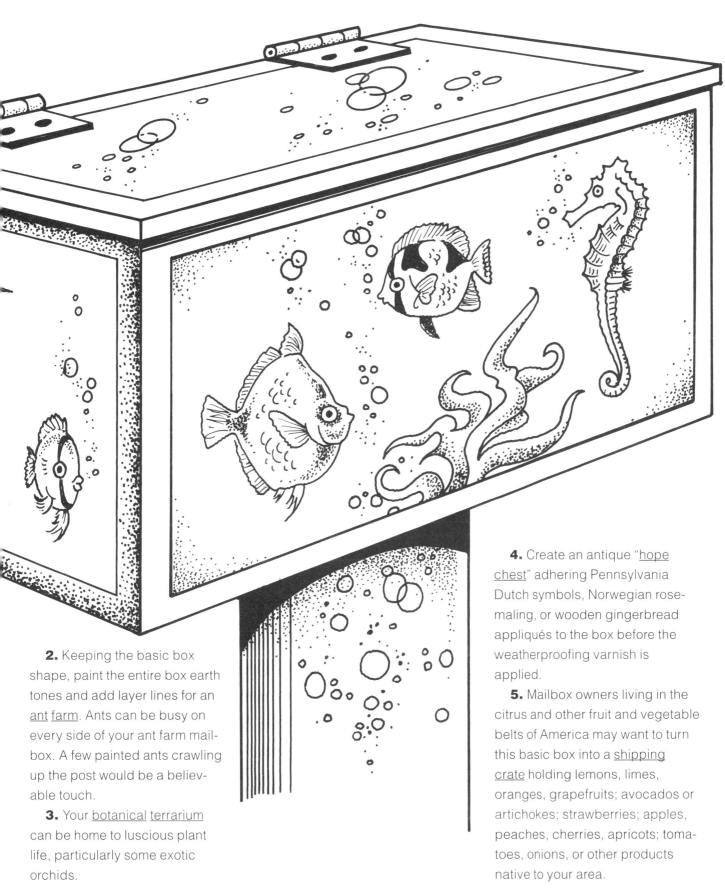

2. Keeping the basic box shape, paint the entire box earth tones and add layer lines for an <u>ant</u> <u>farm</u>. Ants can be busy on every side of your ant farm mailbox. A few painted ants crawling up the post would be a believable touch.

3. Your <u>botanical</u> <u>terrarium</u> can be home to luscious plant life, particularly some exotic orchids.

4. Create an antique "<u>hope chest</u>" adhering Pennsylvania Dutch symbols, Norwegian rosemaling, or wooden gingerbread appliqués to the box before the weatherproofing varnish is applied.

5. Mailbox owners living in the citrus and other fruit and vegetable belts of America may want to turn this basic box into a <u>shipping crate</u> holding lemons, limes, oranges, grapefruits; avocados or artichokes; strawberries; apples, peaches, cherries, apricots; tomatoes, onions, or other products native to your area.

Paint Tube

Basic Box: Paint Tube with Variations

Materials & Tools:

Sheet metal or heavy-gauge
  plastic sheet material
PVC or metal pipe 5" or
  more in diameter and length
Sheet-metal shears, tin snips, or
  metal-cutting equipment
Vice grips or other bending
  tools
Welding equipment or drill with
  bits that can bore holes
  through metal
Bolts or metal screws, washers,
  and nuts
Screwdriver/screws (option)
Hinges
Magnetic door closure or
  other fastener of your choice
Epoxy glue/applicator
Weatherproof paint/brushes

How-to Tips:

1. Draw and transfer a tube pattern and cap piece enlargements onto sheet metal or heavy-gauge plastic sheet material.

2. Cut out the pieces.

3. Attach the pipe to the lid shape to create the tube "cap" that will become the door of the paint-tube mailbox. Use epoxy for PVC, or weld the attachment areas for metal pipe parts and the top of the cap, or attach it to the tube with hinges.

4. Roll the sheet-metal piece for the mailbox into the tube shape, crimping the tail portion and rolling it up two or three times. Weld or epoxy the long seam and the crimped area. Unless welding is the method of attachment, securing the seam and crimped end of the mailbox with bolts or screws is recommended to prevent rupture of those stressed areas over time and adverse weather conditions.

5. Hinge the paint-tube cap/door to the mailbox.

6. Devise a cap door closure that is secure yet easy to open. Standard kitchen cabinet hardware, magnetic or otherwise, is a simple option. Pressure closures such as those found on standard mailboxes will serve well also.

7. Paint the support post to resemble a paintbrush with its ferrule (the metal ring on the shaft of the brush that secures the hairs in place) and perhaps a few fake but believable drips of paint.

8. Paint the tube to resemble the artist's choice of watercolor, acrylic, or oil paint that will proclaim "a painter lives here." Study the label and lid details of any of those types of commercial paint tubes and decorate yours to resemble the appropriate "look."

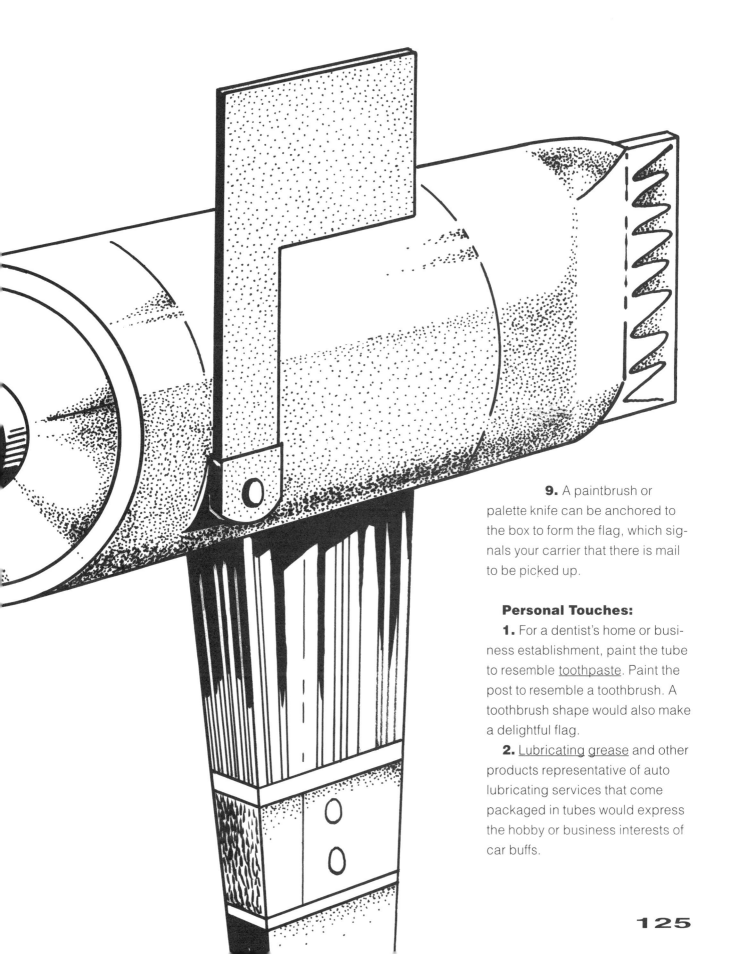

9. A paintbrush or palette knife can be anchored to the box to form the flag, which signals your carrier that there is mail to be picked up.

Personal Touches:

1. For a dentist's home or business establishment, paint the tube to resemble <u>toothpaste</u>. Paint the post to resemble a toothbrush. A toothbrush shape would also make a delightful flag.

2. <u>Lubricating</u> <u>grease</u> and other products representative of auto lubricating services that come packaged in tubes would express the hobby or business interests of car buffs.

125

Crayon Box

Basic Box: Crayon Box
with Variations

Materials & Tools:

Plywood sheets, 1/2" to
  3/4" thick
Saw
Screwdriver/screws
Hammer/nails (option)
Weatherproof paint/brushes
Hinges (2)
Wood glue

How-to Tips:

1. From 1/2"- to-3/4"-thick ply-wood sheets, cut the front and back pieces including the lid parts. Note that the back panel of the mailbox has a narrow lid piece about 1" to 2" high to allow for a pair of hinges and the necessary glue and nails or screws to as-semble the parts. (Experienced woodworkers may want to rabbet the lid to the main box.) The front panel of the box has a lid piece that accounts for approximately one-fourth of the vertical dimen-sion.

2. Cut two rectangles to create the top of the lid and the base of the box, figuring dimensions by the front and back pieces.

3. Cut two side panels, and note that each of them is actually cut into two pieces for the lid and lower portion. There are four pieces altogether that make up the two sides.

4. Assemble with wood glue and nails or screws, making sure the box opens at the top, on an angle, with the hinges at the back.

5. Paint to look like crayons, watercolor markers, or colored pencils.

6. Add a knob or handle on the lid to make receiving the mail much easier for you and your mail carrier.

7. Paint the support post to look like a single crayon, pencil, or marker. Add address and names with paint, and weatherproof with varnish. You may also attach metal numbers and letters with small nails.

Personal Touches:

1. This basic box could become a camera case, binocular case, cereal box, or an electric razor.

2. A television or computer on a stand are options that might be created by clever painters for this basic shape.

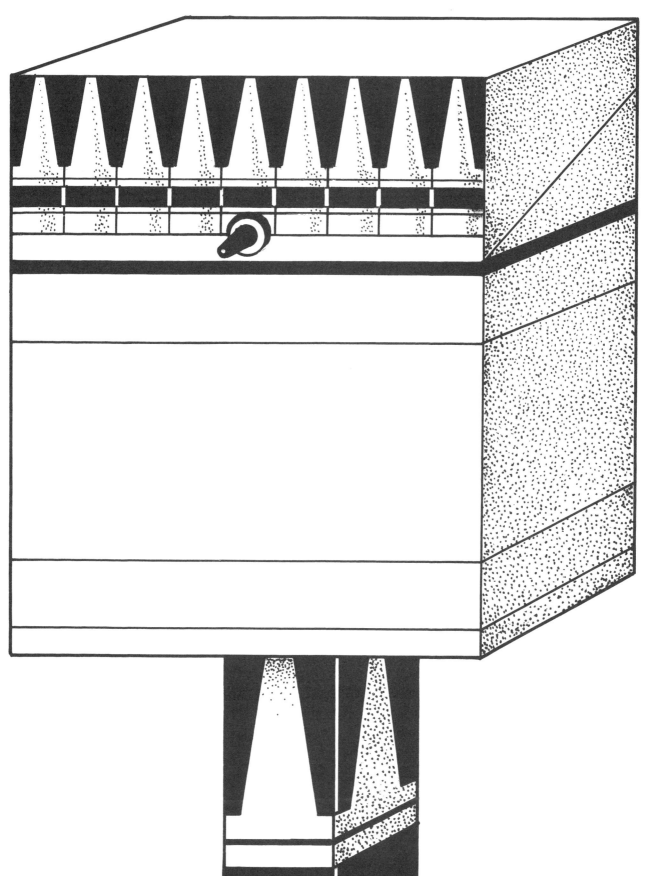

Wedding Cake

Basic Box: Wedding cake
Materials & Tools:

Plywood sheets, 3/4" thick

Electric or handsaw

Hammer/nails (option)

Screwdriver/screws

Wood glue

Handle (grip style)

Hinges (2)

Weatherproof paint/brushes

Wooden boxes of graduated
circular shapes or metal cake
pans (3)

Craft "air hardening" sculpting
material/dough or Perma-Ice ™
tinted with acrylic paint

Pastry bag/decorating tips

Plastic bride and groom, bells,
birds, or other ornaments

See the photo of the Cake Lady®,
Frances Kuyper's, mailbox in the
photo and story section on page 43.

How-to Tips:
Mailbox base

1. Cut 2 pieces of plywood 23-1/2'' by 24" for the top and bottom of the mailbox. The 24" sides will be the sides of the mailbox base; the 23-1/2" sides will be the door and back of the box.

2. Cut 2 pieces of plywood 24" long by 5-1/2" wide to become the sides of the box.

3. Cut 1 piece 23-1/2" long by 5-1/2" wide to become the back of the box.

4. Cut 1 piece 22" long and 5-1/2" wide to become the door of the box. Where you place your box will determine if you hinge it on the left or right side. Affix the hinges and door handle accordingly.

5. Join all of the box pieces with wood glue and nails or screws. Sand any rough spots and wipe clean before painting with two or three coats of weatherproof paint.

Cake tiers

1. On top of the mailbox base, attach 3 circle forms in the manner of cake tiers with epoxy or weatherproof craft glue to form a wedding cake. Inverted cake pans in three sizes will work quite believably.

2. Using spreadable craft material, "ice" the cake and allow to harden.

3. Experiment with a set of cake-decorating tips and soft craft material until you are comfortable with making a variety of scallops, swags, leaves, and roses to complete the cake decorations. Sculpting material can be painted afterward or "dyed" before being pressed through the pastry tip to save painstaking painting later.

4. When the cake is decorated, add all of the weatherproof details you desire: bride and groom, bells, doves, ribbons, metallic leaves, fake pearls, etc.

5. Decoupage or paint the name and address, and a clear indication for where the mail goes, as the Cake Lady® has labeled on the door of her mailbox.

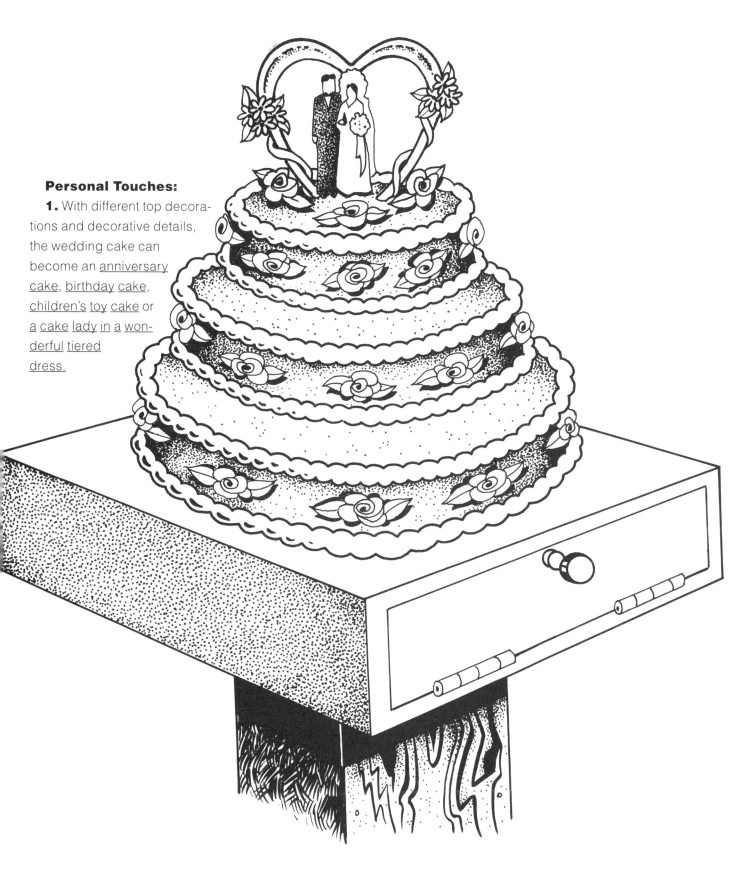

Personal Touches:

1. With different top decorations and decorative details, the wedding cake can become an <u>anniversary</u> <u>cake</u>, <u>birthday</u> <u>cake</u>, <u>children's</u> <u>toy</u> <u>cake</u> or <u>a</u> <u>cake</u> <u>lady</u> <u>in</u> <u>a</u> <u>wonderful</u> <u>tiered</u> <u>dress.</u>

Beer Can Gate

Basic Box: The Beer Can House's Mailbox
Materials & Tools:

Wood framing, 1" x 8"
Electric or handsaw
Hammer/nails
Screwdriver/screws
Beer cans or
   cola cans
Cabinet knobs (2)
Hinges/heavy-gauge wire
Copper sheets .018"
   thick x 1/2" long (2)
Tin snips or metal shears
Brass finishing tacks, Austrian
   rhinestones/clear silicone
   (option)

The Milkovisch's gate/mailbox as seen on page 45 in the photo and story section is a popular tourist attraction in Houston. The entire house is covered with beer cans. These plans only offer tips on the gate containing the mailbox.

How-to Tips:
Gate:

1. Make a gate framework as shown in the illustration from 1" x 8" #1-grade wood. You can build a gate that fills your particular gate width requirements.

2. Lay out the gate parts on a floor or table and fill with cans to make certain all of the long and short rows of cans will fit snugly between the gate framework, allowing for the mailbox shape. Record the number of cans required to fill the space above and below the area where you will secure your mailbox. Then, nail the framework together.

Mailbox:

1. Using 1"x 8" pieces of wood, construct a mailbox. Make the box approximately 15-1/2" wide and 7-3/4" high. You may choose to make the top of the box extend beyond the gate to act as a waterproof shelf over the mailbox door.

2. Attach cabinet knobs or a handle to the door of the mailbox.

3. Join all mailbox pieces with wood glue and nails or screws, except the door.

4. Bend copper-sheet strips to make a latch to hold the door in place. Secure with screws.

5. Ron Milkovisch decorated the mailbox door with letters cut from beer cans and attached the letters with brass finishing tacks. He embellished his mailbox door with Austrian rhinestones held on with clear silicone.

6. Hinge the door to the rest of the mailbox.

Assemble the Gate and the Mailbox Insert:

1. Punch a hole on each side (2 holes per can) of the beer cans. String the rows together on lengths of wire that allow lengths on each end to twist, forming a loop to set a screw into the gate framework. Epoxy glue or clear silicone can be used to further strengthen the joining of one can and one row of cans to another to keep the gate "wall" from sagging over time.

2. Hang the gate frame, and when it is in place, add one row of wired cans at a time with their

round ends facing out. The cans will be lying on their sides. Screw the wire ends into the gate uprights until the fit is tight. Continue adding rows of cans up the gate, creating a wall of cans on which to set the mailbox.

3. Center the mailbox on a row of cans where it will be easy to

reach. Apply epoxy or silicone to the base of the mailbox and the row of cans it sets on to give it stability. Attach the side rows of wired cans to the mailbox and the gate frame on both sides of the mailbox and continue with rows of wired cans the rest of the way up the gate frame, securing wires with screws as you go.

4. Epoxy any joining of the cans if you care to.

5. Seal the mailbox and the wood frame with clear acrylic.

6. Enjoy the stares and comments.

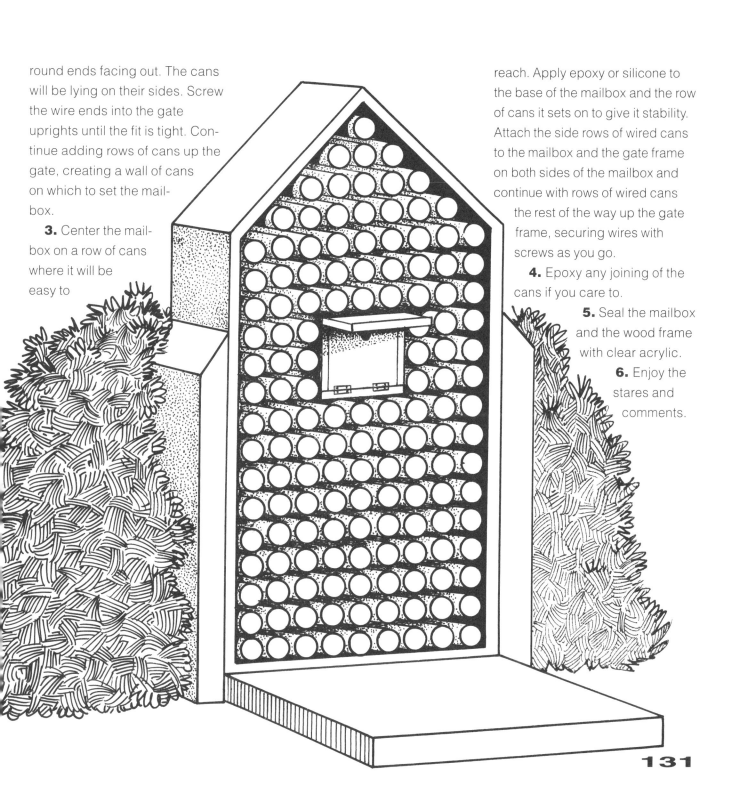

Boot

**Basic Box: Boot
   with Variations**
Materials & Tools:

   Standard rural-delivery mailbox
      secured to a post
   Galvanized stovepipe,
      6" wide x 24" long
   Rivets, sheet-metal screws,
      or bolts
   Sheet-metal sheers or tin snips
   Weatherproof paint/paintbrush
   Epoxy glue

Idea contributed by welding artist Lee Greenberg who built the Flamingo Mailbox pictured in the photo and story section on page 76.

How-to Tips:

1. Cut out and discard "D"-shaped sections from the front and back of one end of the stovepipe to make it fit snugly against the top of the existing mailbox.

2. Attach the stovepipe (which has holes bored near the bottom for moisture to drain, though above where it will attach to the box) to the top rear end of the mailbox with rivets, sheet-metal screws, or through-bolts. Epoxy connecting points.

3. Paint on name, address, and decorative designs, or use decals. Weatherproof.

Personal Touches:

1. The basic boot shape can become a combat boot with the addition of "treads" cut from an old tire and secured to the bottom with screws. Paint black or camouflage style with green, tan, and black. Actual heavy shoestrings can be dipped in liquid decoupage material and "laced" up the front. Paint final shoelace effect with two or three coats of polyurethane to weatherproof.

2. Use decals or paint to make the old woman in the shoe with too many children hanging out of the top and the windows—perfect for a big family or a child-care center.

3. With wide ribbon or strips of cheesecloth folded ragged edges down, wrap the box and the stovepipe "ankle" in the criss-cross manner of ballet shoe ties. Brush with clear-hardening craft goo, allow to dry, paint pink for shoe and laces and white for tights. Weatherproof with two or three coats of polyurethane. This theme is appropriate when the

dancer in the house wants to be famous, even better if the dance school is the mail-receiving site.

4. Cowpokes can alter the top of the stovepipe for the scallops of a hand-tooled, leather cowboy boot. Add a wooden or metal heel and sheet-metal spurs, then paint and weatherproof as above.

5. Create a running or walking shoe with a sock for the athletes in the family. The stovepipe can be painted to resemble a sock, or the adventurously creative can dip a "sock" made of an old towel into craft material, bunch it around the "ankle," allow it to harden, then paint and weatherproof.

6. Nails through the bottom of the box create the cleats of a golf shoe that can be enhanced with a fringed sheet-metal tongue and shoe-string tie, then epoxy for weather-proofing on the inside of the box. Paint the post to resemble a putter. Weatherproof if necessary.

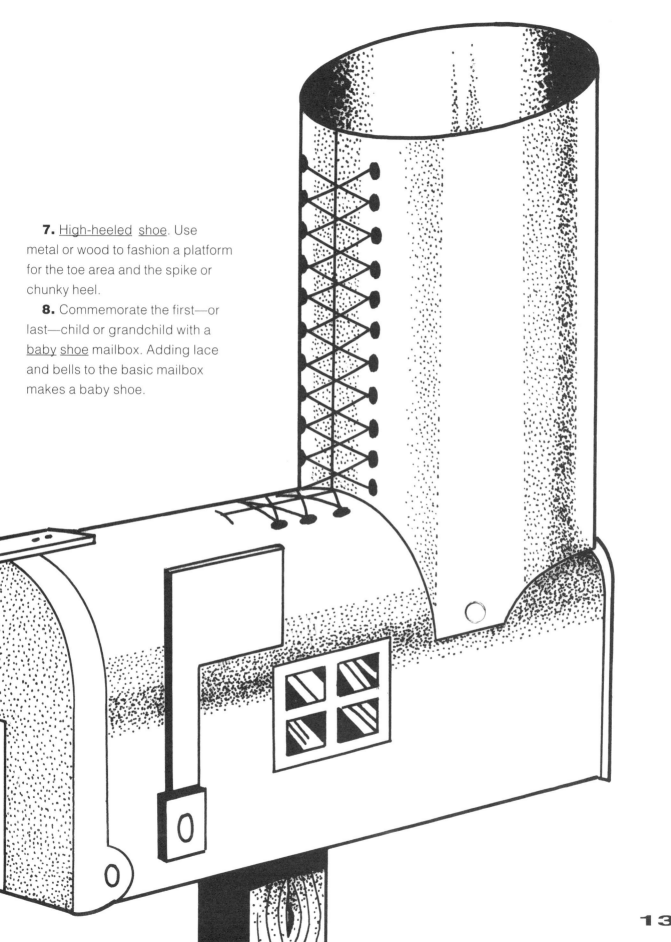

7. <u>High-heeled</u> <u>shoe</u>. Use metal or wood to fashion a platform for the toe area and the spike or chunky heel.

8. Commemorate the first—or last—child or grandchild with a <u>baby</u> <u>shoe</u> mailbox. Adding lace and bells to the basic mailbox makes a baby shoe.

Toolbox

Basic Box: Toolbox with Variations

Materials & Tools:

Plywood sheet, 1/2" thick
Electric or handsaw
Hammer/nails
Screwdriver/screws
Nuts/washers
Wood glue
Hinges (2 or 3)
Handle/bolt attachment, magnetic door closure
Polyurethane varnish
Weatherproof paint/brushes

How-to Tips:

1. Use the shape of the mailbox illustrated to create your basic pattern for door, sides, bottom, and top resembling a toolbox.

2. Cut out all pieces and join front, back, and sides with wood glue and nails or screws.

3. Attach the lid with the number of hinges that seems adequate for the size of box you are building. Use a standard kitchen-cabinet closure, a magnetic one, or other easily operating fixture to keep the door closed.

4. Using a bolt or screw and washer combination, attach the handle to the toolbox.

5. Cut a wrench, hammer, or screwdriver shape from heavy wood. Use your chosen tool to attach to an existing post, or to become the post itself. This illustration allows for the wrench's "bite" to hold newspapers and magazines on dry days.

6. Another tool could become the flag of the mailbox. A ruler, flat level, hammer, etc., would work as a flag that carries out your toolbox theme.

7. Paint your name and address on the mailbox or nail on metal numbers and letters instead. Seal all surfaces with two coats of weatherproof paint or polyurethane varnish.

Personal Touches:

1. With shape and detail adjustments, transform the toolbox into a piece of luggage for the traveler at your house. The addition of a decorative handle on top, luggage wheels on the bottom, and a strap for pulling will enhance the theme of luggage.

2. This shape of box could easily represent a fishing tackle box. Bobbers, flies, reels, fake fish, and other supplies add the necessary theme accents.

3. Many artists and craft hobbyists use toolboxes as art-storage boxes. Vary the "tools" according to what the box holds inside.

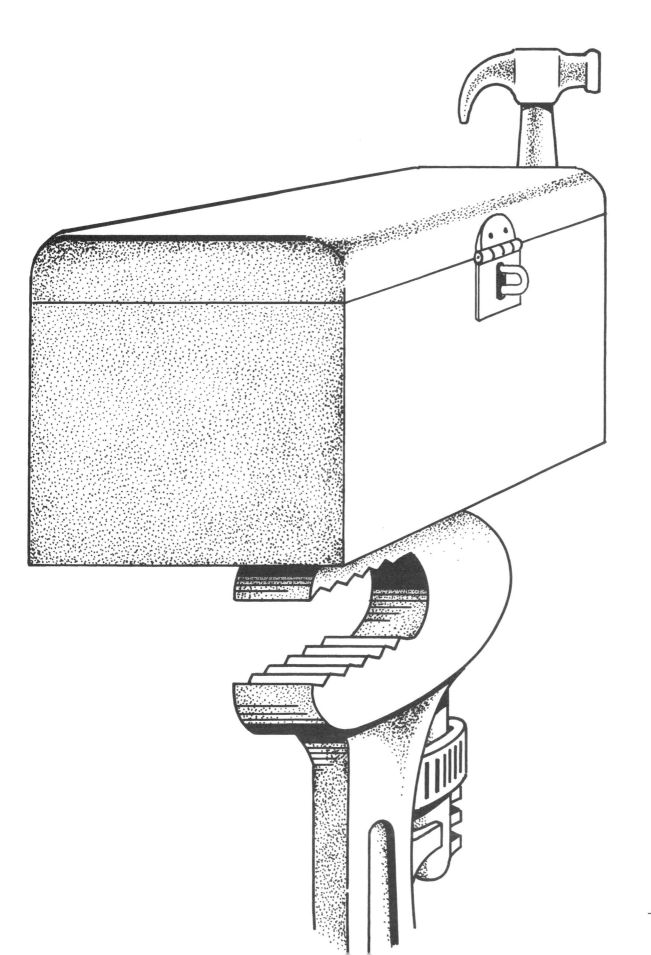

Electrical Outlet

Basic Box:
Electrical Outlet and
Plug with Variations
Materials & Tools:

Plywood sheets, 1/2" to
3/4" thick
Electric or handsaw
Hammer/nails
Screwdriver/screws
Wood glue
Weatherproof paint/brushes
Flat-headed doorknob
(wood or metal), bolt
Hinges (2 or 3)

How-to Tips:

1. Transfer the pattern shapes you design onto a 1/2"-to-3/4"-thick plywood sheet; saw out the shapes.

2. Attach sides to base with wood glue and nails or screws, and then add the top.

3. Measure to find the center of the door panel, mark it, and secure the flat-headed doorknob with a bolt. The knob may be painted first to have a center stripe across its head to resemble a giant screw in the faceplate of an electrical outlet. The outlets to receive the plug prongs may be painted on.

4. Allow wood glue to dry thoroughly before attaching the door with two or three hinges.

5. Paint the post to represent the plug shape in the illustration. Plug should be painted on all four sides of a square post or all the way around a pipe-form post to give the best illusion of an electrical plug from every angle.

6. Keep in mind that plugs and outlets come in many colors. Your choice of colors will be a personal statement that adds to the uniqueness of this unusual idea, perfect for an electrical wizard.

Personal Touches:

1. This box is easily transformed by imaginative painting into a refrigerator or upright freezer, particularly an antique one; a microwave oven; cooking range; safe for valuables; television; stacked entertainment center containing tape, CD player, AM/FM radio, amplifier panel, etc.; a washer or dryer; computer CPU unit with painted-on CD and floppy-disk ports.

2. For an apartment building or brownstone with windows, steps painted up the mailbox door, potted plants painted on a stoop, a cat in the window, and a clothes-line pegged with drying laundry on the sides could add to the whimsey of high-rise living on your mailbox.

3. By replacing the doorknob "screw" in the faceplate of this electrical outlet with a wooden "switch" in the same spot on the mailbox door, the electrical outlet may be transformed into a light switch. Paint the faceplate (door of the mailbox) to resemble a switch plate in your home or in a hardware store. For those plates that have decorative shapes, or stencil patterns, paint can do the trick.

4. A see-through <u>toy</u> <u>box</u> can be created with paint or decals. The toys don't have to be just for children. Boats, golf clubs, tennis rackets, and so forth could be "seen" through the sides of a "plexiglass" box. To enhance the illusion of this mailbox being a clear plastic toy box, paint two coats of clear polyurethane varnish over the entire surface for the shiny effect of plexiglass. Adding "for effect only" hinges to the top for a toy-box-lid appearance could add to the credibility of the box, or use the basic box from the crayon mailbox plan in the first place. Using a wooden "toy" bolted on for the doorknob would add a delightful touch. Wooden toys include cars, animals, airplanes, boats, sports equipment, monsters, trains, and more.

5. The clear storage box idea could have "stacks" of folded quilt fabric in a <u>sewing</u> <u>box</u>. Other variations would be a <u>yarn</u> <u>storage</u> <u>box</u> for handicrafters.

6. For the family that loves reading and collecting books, the small-town library, or the independent bookstore owner, painting this rectangular mailbox to resemble a <u>bookcase</u> full of books is a way of promoting reading as a pleasurable and informative pastime.

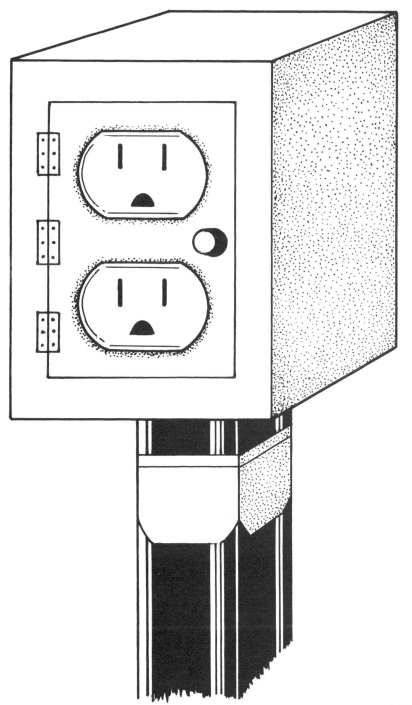

Cellular Phone

Basic Box:
  Portable/Cellular Phone
  with Variations
Materials & Tools:

  Plywood sheet, 1/2" to
    3/4" thick
  Electric or handsaw
  Hammer/nails
  Screwdriver/screws (option)
  Drill/bits or jigsaw
  Wood glue/epoxy
  Hinges (2 or 3)
  PVC pipe/cap
  Weatherproof paint/brushes
  Polyurethane varnish
  Doorknob/magnetic fasteners

How-to Tips:

1. Transfer patterns you design to your choice of plywood sheets. The larger you make your mailbox proportions, the thicker you will want to have your wood parts.

2. Cut out the required number of pieces. Save scraps to cut small squares that become the "touch tone" numbers on the portable phone.

3. Drill or use a jigsaw to cut a hole the size of the diameter of PVC pipe you have selected to be the antenna of your mailbox phone.

4. Join all pieces with wood glue and nails or screws. Make the inside shelf that will hold the mail secure with wood biscuits; it isn't necessary unless your mailbox receives heavy packages.

5. Hinge the door to the mailbox. It may open from the top or the bottom. If hinged from the bottom, magnetic fasteners at the top will hold the door in place against gravity.

6. Attach the antenna with epoxy for both security and to weatherproof the attachment that could leak water onto your mail in a heavy rain or sustained snow build up.

7. Painted "holes" or screws can give the appearance of the speaker without making real holes that put the mail in jeopardy of being damaged.

8. Glue on the buttons for dialing. Decal numbers may be decoupaged onto these "keys" with clear polyurethane varnish.

Personal Touches:

1. For a duplex, a home with children, or a house with an apartment, put up a pair of these portable-phone mailboxes, change the features, and paint the buttons a hot color such as those found on children's toys to transform them into walkie talkies.

138

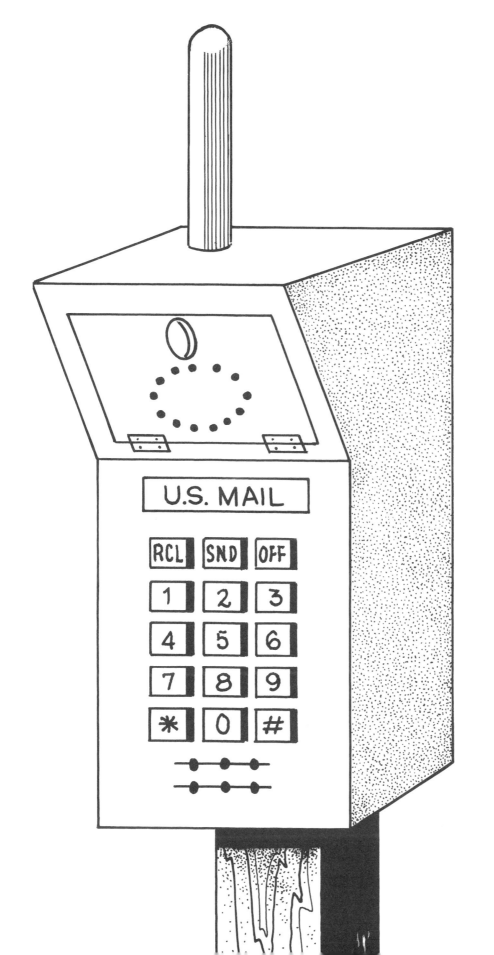

Train

Basic Box:
Train with Variations
Materials & Tools:

Standard rural-delivery
    mailbox secured to a post
Clear polyurethane varnish/
    disposable sponge brush
Weatherproof paint/brushes

How-to Tips:

1. On a copy machine, or by hand, enlarge a train design to fit your mailbox.

2. Paint the image of a train directly onto the mailbox.

3. Paint the flag that comes on your mailbox to match the striped effect in this illustraton. Masking or drafting (easy pull-off) tape will help make the lines straight and an equal distance apart. Varnish with clear polyurethane. **Do not varnish the inner joint of the flag where it attaches to the box or it will not move up and down when dry.**

Personal Touches:

1. Train buffs may prefer to design their train shape after a particular <u>classic</u> <u>model</u>, even an <u>antique</u> or <u>toy</u> <u>train</u>. Library and other resource books as well as models and toy trains may be your inspiration. You may also consult the Resource Guide to Mailbox Artists on page 110 to arrange for a one-of-a-kind painted mailbox.

2. <u>Sixteen</u>-<u>wheeler</u> <u>transport</u> <u>trucks</u>, <u>flat</u>-<u>bed</u> <u>trucks</u>, <u>airplanes</u>, <u>submarines</u>, <u>naval</u> <u>aircraft</u> <u>carriers</u>, and numerous other long-like-a-mailbox vehicles are exciting options easily adapted to mailbox art. Many clip-art books have "free to copy" designs that can serve as the pattern for your choice of a vehicle mailbox.

3. An old-fashioned <u>circus-train</u> <u>car</u> or <u>wagon</u> would be just the ticket for a big family with lots of pets or for a child-care center. Adding images of exotic animals, fancy boxcars, and bright colors will create the illusion of the days when the circus train brought the whole town to the tracks to watch the unloading of the animals and the elephants that helped put up the big tent.

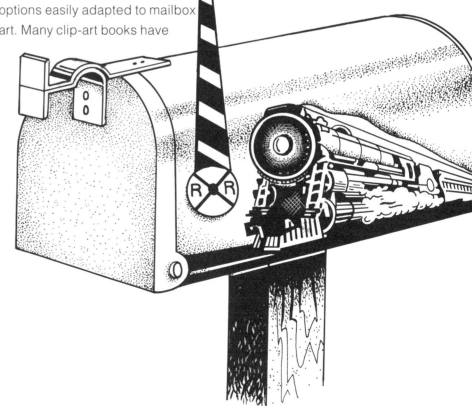

Stamps

Basic Box:
Stamp Collector's
Mailbox with Variations
Materials & Tools:

Standard rural-delivery
mailbox secured to a post
Canceled or new
postage stamps (option)
Craft glue or clear
polyurethane varnish
Scissors and brushes
Paint/brushes (option)

How-to Tips:

1. Collect and cut out your favorite postage stamps, close to their perforated edges or enlarge and paint your own favorite stamps.

2. Turn them upside down and apply craft glue or clear polyurethane varnish to secure the stamps to the mailbox. Use the unprinted side of a piece of paper bag as your gluing surface. Newspaper ink comes off and can destroy the face of your stamps, but a grocery bag's inside surface is sturdy enough to remain flat and provide a clean area to work. Tape a piece to your worktable. When the glue or varnish step is finished, simply roll it up and throw it away.

3. One at a time, place the stamps randomly or in a repeat pattern onto the mailbox. Press into place, overlapping or not, as you choose. Smooth firmly to remove all air bubbles underneath.

4. Apply number and letter decals or press-on letters for your name and address. Subtitle with "philatelist" for fun.

5. Brush the entire box with two coats of clear polyurethane varnish, allowing for drying time in between.
Apply a fresh

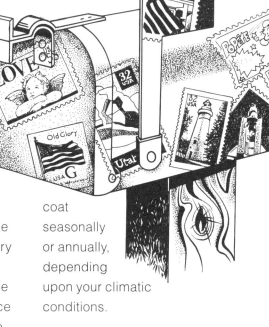

coat
seasonally
or annually,
depending
upon your climatic
conditions.

Personal Touches:

1. Select stamps with themes for your favorite hobby or a topic that tells something about you, such as <u>trains</u>, <u>steamships</u>, <u>bicycles</u>, <u>wildflowers</u>, <u>birds</u>, <u>endangered species</u>, <u>carousel horses</u>, <u>jazz</u> and <u>blues performers</u>, etc. <u>American flags</u> or <u>W.W.II</u> stamps are perfect for the patriot and veteran. <u>Marilyn Monroe</u>, <u>Elvis Presley</u>, <u>Ella Fitzgerald</u>, <u>U.S.</u> <u>presidents</u>, or any <u>hero</u> or <u>heroine</u> that suits your fancy and has become the subject of a stamp series makes a perfect theme for your mailbox.

2. <u>Foreign stamps</u> or colorful <u>foreign money</u> (low denominations to discourage theft) express the interests of those with relatives or pen pals around the globe. World travelers will enjoy this easy and informative way to say where they've been. Cruise stickers and foreign country decals are other options. Your mailbox may even be painted to look like a piece of <u>luggage</u>. Add painted or actual handles, zippers, tags, wheels, destination stickers, and designer "labels."

Mail Truck

Basic Box: Wooden truck secured to a post.

Materials & Tools:

Plywood sheets, 1/2" to
 3/4" thick
Hammer/nails
Screwdriver/screws
Weatherproof paint/brushes
Wheels
Wood glue/epoxy

How-to Tips:

1. Cut two plywood sides appropriate for the length you want your mailbox to be.

2. Cut three rectangular panels of plywood for the hood and front window of the truck of the width you want the truck to be.

3. Cut a back door to fit. (This will be where the mail goes in and is taken out. The opening must face the road for your mail carrier.)

It may be two doors, or a single door. Attach with two or four hinges.

4. Cut a base to extend from the front end to the tail end of the truck. Join all pieces to form the truck mailbox and use both wood glue and nails or screws to make a tight, weatherproof box.

5. Attach recycled toy wheels or model-car wheels with screws, nails, or epoxy glue.

6. Paint the truck white and add a red-and-blue-stripe design under the windows to make a U.S. Postal Service mail-delivery truck. Follow the stripe design placement on the mail truck mailbox in the photo sections of this book, or observe the mail trucks in your community.

7. The U.S. Postal Service eagle-head logo would add a finishing touch to your mail-truck mailbox.

Personal Touch:

1. Attach bicycle reflectors for head- and taillights.

2. A standard red, metal mail flag would be a color-coordinating natural on this box.

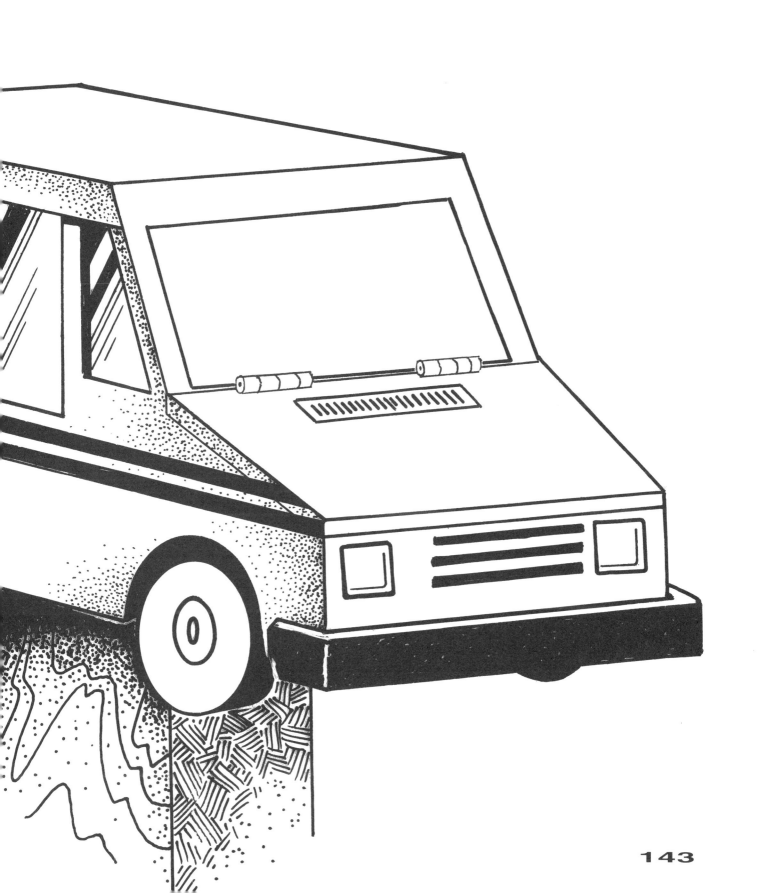